Completing Dissertations in the Behavioral Sciences and Education

A Systematic Guide for Graduate Students

Thomas J. Long
John J. Convey
Adele R. Chwalek

Completing Dissertations in the Behavioral Sciences and Education

Jossey-Bass Publishers • San Francisco

COMPLETING DISSERTATIONS IN THE BEHAVIORAL SCIENCES
AND EDUCATION
A Systematic Guide for Graduate Students
by Thomas J. Long, John J. Convey, and Adele R. Chwalek

Copyright © 1985 by: Jossey-Bass Inc., Publishers
350 Sansome Street
San Francisco, California 94104

Library of Congress Cataloging in Publication Data

Long, Thomas J. (date)
  Completing dissertations in the behavioral sciences
and education.

  (The Jossey-Bass higher education series) (The
Jossey-Bass social and behavioral science series)
    Bibliography: p. 193
    Includes index.
    1. Dissertations, Academic. 2. Psychology—Research—
Methodology. 3. Education—Research—Methodology.
4. Proposal writing in research. I. Convey, John J.
(date). II. Chwalek, Adele R. (date).
III. Title. IV. Series. V. Series: Jossey-Bass social
and behavioral science series.
LB2369.L65   1985   808'.042'071173   85-45063
ISBN 0-87589-658-8 (alk. paper)

Manufactured in the United States of America

JACKET DESIGN BY WILLI BAUM

FIRST EDITION
HB Printing   10 9 8 7 6 5

Code 8539

A joint publication in
The Jossey-Bass
Higher Education Series
and
The Jossey-Bass
Social and Behavioral Science Series

Preface

Nearly all doctoral programs in the behavioral sciences and education require a dissertation, and a great many masters' programs require a thesis as a prerequisite for graduation. Unfortunately, many degree candidates fail to focus on the particulars of writing a thesis or dissertation until very late in their graduate careers. The result is often an upsetting scramble to select a suitable topic, review the literature associated with it, and produce a proposal and final product before a university-imposed time limit expires.

Sadder still, many capable students never finish their degrees because they focus their attention on everything but their dissertations or theses. They complete their course work without considering how the individual courses fit together to form a whole. They do not develop an area of concentration over which they have thorough mastery. They fail to consider or understand the intricacies of the dissertation process. All too many students finally give up seeking a degree because they cannot integrate all the aspects of their learning into a final product —yet most of these students could have and should have completed their degrees.

Purpose of This Book

Completing Dissertations in the Behavioral Sciences and Education is designed to help students finish the degrees for which they enroll in college. It attempts to systematically reinforce critical steps in the dissertation process that directors and instructors often introduce unsystematically. These steps include presenting a clearly articulated and reasonable timeline for completing a degree, selecting and developing a suitable topic, developing and expressing hypotheses and research questions, determining when and how to conduct pilot studies, and selecting the most appropriate methods for collecting data and analyzing and reporting findings. *Completing Dissertations* is also designed to inform students about problems their instructors, advisers, and directors may not discuss with them; for example, how to deal with the lack of continuous structure in graduate education; how to cope with family upset, financial difficulties, or difficulties with faculty members; where to look for financial help; and how to make best use of statisticians, editors, and translators.

This book outlines, in more or less chronological order, the steps students must take to complete the thesis or dissertation efficiently and effectively, beginning with the choice of a suitable topic and concluding with the final oral defense. It is not intended to either provide or replace a good manual on style, a thorough understanding of research methods or statistics, a firm grounding in one's major, or general scholarly ability. Rather, it is like a road map; it points the way to a particular town, but it does not offer driving lessons or tips on automobile repair.

Completing Dissertations was written by scholars in the behavioral sciences and education and should therefore be of special interest to students in the fields of psychology, education, and social work. Its content should also be applicable to those studying nursing and other health sciences with a behavioral base, certain aspects of anthropology, criminal justice, and even linguistics. We feel that the relatively precise focus of this book on the behavioral disciplines has allowed us to provide a more comprehensive and penetrating review of applicable resources than might have been possible in a book with a wider view, yet it has not destroyed the general utility of the book as a dissertation guide.

Completing Dissertations can be used as the principal text in courses intended to guide students through the process of doing a dissertation or thesis. (Most of the advice given regarding dissertations applies to theses as well.) It may also be used as a supplementary text in seminars that introduce students to the process of obtaining a graduate degree or in research methods courses, particularly those in the behavioral sciences and education.

Overview of the Contents

Chapter One identifies common obstacles that may impede a student's progress toward a completed dissertation and a degree. These obstacles include financial hardship; competition for time among studies, job, and family; problems of attitude, such as taking one's work too lightly; receiving too little positive reinforcement for work completed; and the lack of skills to carry out necessary research. It also offers suggestions about ways to overcome these obstacles.

Chapter Two tells how to go about selecting and developing a researchable topic. It suggests that students begin their search for a suitable dissertation or thesis topic at the outset of their graduate programs. The characteristics of a good research topic—including whether it is sufficiently delimited, significant, unique, of personal interest, and feasible in terms of the student's time, ability, and other resources—and a preferred approach to uncovering such a topic are also outlined here.

Chapter Three presents information on the use of library services, materials, and personnel. It describes how library materials can help in selecting and defining a research topic and how to review the literature associated with the topic chosen. In addition, this chapter lists the most useful bibliographic resources for the behavioral sciences and education and provides an extensive review of the best available computer search services and data bases.

Chapter Four discusses issues students should consider in selecting a dissertation director and advisory committee. These issues include the standing of the committee members in the professional community, their interest in the topic, their accessibility, the seriousness with which they approach the dissertation process, and the goodness of fit between the student and the director, and other committee members. It also suggests the most productive ways for students to interact with these committee members.

Chapters Five and Six outline the organization and writing of the dissertation proposal, providing specific guidance about what to include in each section. Special emphasis is placed on quantitative research studies. Chapter Five covers the proposal's introductory and review-of-literature chapter, and Chapter Six describes the method chapter.

Chapter Seven outlines the usual procedures for getting a proposal approved. It indicates how students should conduct themselves during a proposal defense, how to handle proposal revisions, and how to make changes in one's committee if that becomes necessary.

Chapter Eight discusses the professional aids available to students and the ethics of using them. Aids covered include computers and statistical software packages, as well as public servants, editors, translators, statisticians, and other consultants. The chapter briefly considers ethics questions related to the use of human and animal subjects and to copyrights.

Chapter Nine outlines the structure of the dissertation itself, emphasizing the importance of producing an accurate and scholarly dissertation. It spells out how to update the proposal, how to give a complete accounting of results obtained, and how to discuss and evaluate these results.

Chapter Ten describes the final oral defense. It offers advice on how to prepare for the defense, how students should act during it, and how final defenses are usually conducted. It explains how decisions are made by defense committees and what students should do after a decision has been reached.

Appendix A is a detailed timeline, in graphic form, showing all the stages of the dissertation process as they are usually scheduled, and giving the student an overview of the entire process in sequence. It should prove an excellent planning aid.

Appendix B provides a brief description of the six types of research most commonly found in dissertations. It shows how the format and other suggestions given in this book might apply to each research type.

Appendix C offers a list of bibliographic resources not otherwise mentioned in the text. The list covers directories of funding sources, including on-line data bases of funding sources; style manuals; and statistical manuals.

We believe that students will find this a useful book to read early in their graduate program. It is intended to help them focus their program of study efficiently and to assist them in avoiding pitfalls that might slow or even halt their progress. Students should also find it a handy guide and reference as they move from stage to stage of the actual production of a dissertation or thesis.

A number of scholars in various universities have reviewed this manuscript. We are grateful to all of them. We also wish to extend special thanks to Mary Kay Winner and Margaret Brooks, who assisted in the preparation of the manuscript, and to the many students from whom we have learned so much about the dissertation process.

Washington, D.C.   Thomas J. Long
July 1985   John J. Convey
                                            Adele R. Chwalek

Contents

The Authors

Thomas J. Long is associate professor of education at The Catholic University of America. He received his B.A. degree (1960) from St. Meinrad College in philosophy and his M.A. (1966) and Ed.D. (1968) degrees from Arizona State University in counselor education. He has served as the acting chairman of the Department of Educational Psychology at the University of Illinois, Champaign-Urbana, and as coordinator of the program in counseling at The Catholic University of America.

A licensed psychologist, Long is nationally known for his research on latchkey children. He currently serves as the president of the National Institute for Latchkey Children and Youth, a not-for-profit public corporation based in Washington, D.C. Long is a member of the American Association for Counseling and Development and the American Association of Marriage and Family Therapists.

John J. Convey is associate professor of education at The Catholic University of America. He received his B.A. degree (1962) from LaSalle College in mathematics, his M.Sc. degree (1968) from Ohio State University in mathematics, and his Ph.D. degree (1974) from Florida State University in education. He has extensive experience as an adviser of students, having directed more than twenty-five doctoral dissertations in the past ten years. Convey's main research activities have concerned statistical and measurement issues involved with the determination of the effectiveness of schools and with human development. He is a member of the American Educational Research Association, the National Catholic Educational Association, the National Council for Measurement in Education, and the Psychometric Society.

Adele R. Chwalek is a librarian at The Catholic University of America. She received her B.A. degree (1967) from the College of St. Catherine in library science and her M.S.L.S. (1972) from The Catholic University of America.

Chwalek has served as a catalogue librarian, and as a reference and liaison librarian for education and psychology, and is currently circulation librarian and project manager for automation at The Catholic University of America Libraries. She has taught library use to students on graduate and undergraduate levels, developed a program of bibliographic instruction for students in education and psychology, and lectured on bibliographic instruction at regional and national conferences.

Completing
Dissertations in the
Behavioral Sciences
and Education

A Systematic Guide
for Graduate Students

 ONE

Overcoming Obstacles to Completing Dissertations

Eileen had done excellent work in her graduate courses and had passed her comprehensive exam with flying colors . . . but that was five years ago. Her dissertation still lay on her desk, uncompleted. When friends asked her about it, she sighed, "I really should get back to it, but I just never seem to have the time. I'm a housewife now, you know, and we do a lot of entertaining for my husband's business customers, so I'm busy. Besides, there are a few more tests I want to run on my data. My writing needs polishing, too. My dissertation just isn't ready yet." Eileen's friends suspected that it would never be.

Vivian, too, had a busy schedule. Like Eileen, she was married. Her husband's income was not high, so Vivian had to work part time to help support their family, which included a baby daughter. Yet she was determined to finish the dissertation she had started two years ago. She planned her schedule carefully so that she was able to spend a few hours on it every week, but she knew that wasn't enough. After investigating many possibilities, she applied for and won a grant offered by a baby food manufacturer to a student doing research in childhood nutrition. The grant was not large, but it was enough to let Vivian quit her job and devote most of her time to her research. As a bonus, she saw more of her daughter, too.

1

Of all the steps in the expensive and time-consuming process of obtaining an advanced degree, the thesis or dissertation is often the most difficult and challenging. Most students take between nine and eighteen months to finish a dissertation; but some dissertations have been completed in six months, while others are not finished in six years.

Most graduate programs provide students with the guidance of at least one faculty adviser and with adequate time to complete the work. However, the blending of skills and knowledge into an acceptable final product is ultimately the student's responsibility. You must finish your dissertation on your own initiative, talents, and timetable.

A number of variables, unforeseen obstacles, and fortuitous events may affect that timetable. Many of these problems and their solutions do not relate to the actual task of writing the dissertation and are therefore outside the scope of this book. We can, however, make you aware of some common obstacles and aids to the dissertation process in the hope that, forewarned, you will be able to confront and surmount the obstacles and take advantage of the aids, thereby smoothing the path to your degree.

Most obstacles to successful completion of a dissertation fall into one of three categories. Some obstacles are external problems, such as financial hardship or competition for time among studies, job, and family. Others are problems of attitude, such as a tendency to make excuses or a desire to spend too little time—or too much—in hard work. A third category of obstacles relates to the lack of study or professional skills, such as skills of time management or of writing. In this chapter we will look at the most common obstacles in each of these categories and suggest ways of dealing with them.

External Problems

Financial Hardship. The financial burdens of dissertation research, possibly coupled with family or other needs, can be formidable obstacles—but they need not bring your degree program to a standstill. A combination of research to discover loan possibilities and creative thinking about other ways to produce income can solve most financial problems.

If you are suffering financial hardship while working on your dissertation, consult your school's financial aid officer at least once a semester to make sure you are informed of all sources of aid available to you. Don't assume, however, that the financial aid officer will be aware of every source of support for which you are eligible. Be ready to do your own research. For example, review your family's background to find out whether there are scholarships for which you might be eligible because a member of your family was, say, an officer in the Daughters of the American Revolution or the Knights of Columbus.

Check publications such as the *College Blue Book: Scholarships, Fellowships, Grants and Loans,* revised biannually by the Macmillan Company, for sources of support that may apply to you. There you can find such interesting awards as the eighty-six renewable grants offered by the Spencer Foundation for study in the behavioral sciences or education; forty awards ranging from $2,000 to $15,000 per academic year, renewable for two years, offered by the Doctoral Dissertation and Small Grants Research Projects Program, Employment and Training Division of the Department of Labor; Fellowships for Doctoral Research in Employment and Training, sponsored by the Social Science Research Council; Japanese American Citizens' League Awards, including scholarships, fellowships, and grants; the annual grant awarded by the National Association of University Women; and the Klingenstein Fellowships for graduate research and study by teachers employed in private or independent schools.

Find out about the availability of student loans. Money from such loans can take the worst of the pinch out of an otherwise tight budget. The Guaranteed Student Loan Program currently provides loans of $5,000 per year up to a maximum of $25,000 at a rate of interest below normal bank rates. Best of all, interest does not begin to accrue, nor do you start paying back these loans, until six months after you graduate. You then have ten years to pay back the entire sum.

There are other loan programs as well. For example,

Auxiliary Loans to Assist Students (ALAS) allows you to borrow up to $3,000 per year, but interest begins to accrue as soon as you receive the money, and you must begin paying back the money after a six-month grace period. The ALAS program might be exceptionally useful for short-term emergencies or to finance the later stages of your dissertation.

Check your own university's loan possibilities, too. For short-term financial needs, universities or even individual departments are often able to make small loans. Such loans are usually under $1,000 and must be paid back within a year, often at or below the prevailing interest rate. In addition, some universities conduct their own long-term loan programs. They may use endowment funds to provide loans at low interest.

Don't overlook your program adviser or dissertation director as a referral source for financial help. An adviser or department head often knows about part-time jobs on campus or in the nearby community. Advisers may also know of sources for direct student funding.

Another approach is to look at your dissertation itself as a possible source of income: In other words, try to get a grant to do your research. This is what Vivian did in our opening example. If you begin thinking about this possibility at the outset of your program, you should be able to locate potential funding sources and design your dissertation research in time to apply for a grant. Investigate government agencies, private philanthropic organizations, and businesses as grant sources.

If you plan to seek grants, begin this activity early in your graduate program, since you will have to plan your proposal well in advance of actually beginning to collect data for it. Once you have a general idea of your dissertation subject, look carefully at your topic and possible sources for funding in order to decide whether funding is likely. If chances seem slight, efforts to obtain outside funds may not be worth the time they will take.

If you are willing to be a little flexible about your dissertation subject, look for topics of interest to you that are also of general public interest or of special interest to a particular funding source. Keep a log of important or popular topics you encounter in professional journals and see whether any of them match your interests.

Next, review funding source directories, such as those listed in Appendix C, at the end of this book, to look for sources of funds compatible with your area of research. In addition to the *College Blue Book,* the *Annual Register of Grant Support, The Foundation Directory* (1981), and the *Grants Register* (1984) may be particularly helpful.

Generally, grants are obtained on the basis of a proposal to the funding source. Obtain specific proposal instructions from each source that seems to be promising. Equipped with this information and in consultation with your adviser or department head, you can then begin to put together a proposal for funding. We recommend that you consult Bauer's (1984) *The How-To Grants Manual: Successful Grantseeking Techniques for Obtaining Public and Private Grants.* This useful manual leads you through the process of preparing a proposal one step at a time.

Be warned that developing a proposal takes time and effort, followed by patience while the proposal goes through the process of review and approval. Developing a proposal and waiting to obtain funding can easily take a year, sometimes more— another important reason for starting the process early.

You should also note that grants seldom come without restrictions. If the demands of the funding source do not exactly coincide with your own research plans, you may be confronted with the choice of adjusting your research focus to meet the source's requirements or losing the funding.

Despite these obstacles, outside funding is often a worthwhile goal to pursue. Not only will a research grant help to defray the cost of your study, but you will learn something about "grantsmanship" in the process of looking for funds. This experience can serve you well in your later career.

Conflict Between Study and Job. Accepting a full-time job, whether because of financial need or a desire to get involved in the practice of your profession, may interfere with the completion of your thesis or dissertation. The better and more marketable your skills, the better the job you may be offered.

Many students find such predissertation jobs very appealing and conclude that, since they "have only the dissertation to do," they can handle both the job and the dissertation. A few can—but most can't. It has been clearly shown that students with full-time jobs take longer to finish—and more of them do not complete their dissertations—than do students who concentrate their full energies on completing their degrees. Even a part-time job can cause problems, as Vivian found in our opening example, especially if it is combined with family responsibilities. Here's a good rule of thumb: When you begin the serious job of writing your proposal, you should be prepared to allocate no less than twenty hours each week to your dissertation or thesis until you have completed the whole process.

If you feel that you must take a job, plan a schedule that will allow sufficient time for your family, job, and dissertation before accepting the post. You should also discuss your plans with your employer before you make a final decision. Employers are often quite understanding about the demands imposed by a graduate program and may be willing to make allowances for your studies if they have been informed of your plans in advance. If, after following these steps, you come to believe that you will not be able to complete your dissertation and hold this particular job at the same time, or that your family life, your health, or the quality of your work will suffer if you try, you should probably reevaluate the importance of this job in light of the sacrifices it demands.

If you are already working full time, talk with your employer about ways to reduce your work load in order to have more time available for conducting your research. For example, you might seek a temporary leave without pay, ask to reduce the number of hours you regularly work, use accumulated vacation time, or be given some paid allowance time by your employer. You should also check whether your employer has a regular policy of supporting graduate study as part of a company benefits package. Finally, try to avoid accepting new responsibilities or a new position while you are working on your dissertation or thesis.

The best kind of job to hold while working on your dissertation is probably one on campus, such as an assistantship or a position in a residence hall or the library. These positions are usually poorly paid, but they can at least keep you going while letting you stay close to the tools and materials you are likely to need for your dissertation. Combining a part-time campus job with student loans can allow you to pay your bills and still pursue your degree program with a minimum of disturbance.

Family Problems. Marital and family responsibilities do not cease because you are writing a dissertation. When these responsibilities increase, as with a pregnancy, an illness in your family, or marital discord, work on your dissertation can be seriously disrupted.

If your family needs more of your time, try to rearrange your schedule to provide the extra time for family concerns. If the problem is serious enough to demand your full attention, take a leave of absence from your studies. It is better to resolve a serious family problem and then return with renewed vigor to your education than to try, and be unable, to deal with both simultaneously. If family problems are severe enough to require outside help, seek family counseling. Many universities provide this service to enrolled students.

Problems of Attitude

Excuses. Excuses probably impede more dissertations than any other factor. Unlike real obstacles, excuses are self-made. They are neither honest choices nor well-grounded reasons for difficulty; rather, they are usually a self-deceptive way to disguise choices for which we do not wish to accept responsibility. We may erect excuses because we fear to examine our true situation or motivations or because we fear that someone else will disagree with our choices and penalize us for them.

Many situations in graduate school can tempt a student to create excuses. A student named Stuart, for example, failed his first try at a comprehensive exam. He bemoaned his lack of intellectual ability and praised the talents of his peers to the skies. This academic breast-beating kept him from facing the fact that he did not choose to spend the time and energy that was needed to pass that exam. Excuses were one of Eileen's problems in our opening example, too.

Suppose your dissertation director leaves to accept a post at another university or you discover that you have hypertension. Either of these occurrences could offer you a ready excuse for ending your program of study prematurely. Almost any student can find at least one substantial excuse for not completing a dissertation or graduate school. "I'm too broke, busy, sick, stupid, worried, old, or young." "My family short-changed me, pampered me, didn't demand enough from me, or demanded too much from me." "My wife or husband, my kids, the economy"—nearly anything can be used to justify not achieving a goal. If you tend to make excuses, learn to recognize them for what they are and to analyze them, especially those that you repeat. They may offer valuable clues to the real pressures and anxieties that keep you from completing your work.

Some students need professional help in overcoming an excuse habit. Seek out such help, if you need it. Most universities provide psychological services for students at little or no cost. If you find yourself bogged down in your pursuit of a degree and merely making excuses for your lack of progress, use any means necessary to find the real problem and correct it.

Lack of Commitment. Having too little respect for the planning, dedication, and work demanded by a dissertation or thesis can cause some students—often the brightest ones—to fail to complete their degrees. These are the students who have grown accustomed to "sliding" their way through school. They dash out course papers at the last minute and still receive acceptable grades. When they try the same strategy on their dissertation or thesis, however, they fail. Advisory committee members are usually very sensitive to hasty or careless work and respond to it with annoyance.

If you have never had to work hard in school before, you must prepare to do so now. Accept the fact that a dissertation or thesis will demand more of your talent and time than any other project you undertake during your degree program. Plan to give this work the commitment of time and energy that its importance deserves.

Excessive Commitment. Taking work too seriously can be as much of a barrier as not taking it seriously enough. Writing a thesis or dissertation is indeed serious work, but some students so inflate the importance of what they are doing that they never seem to relax. They run in constant hyperdrive, worrying themselves and everyone around them to distraction.

Sometimes this overserious aggressiveness is the product of what is commonly referred to as a "Type A" personality. "Type A" has become the national slang for the harried, hostile, achievement-obsessed personalities who champ and bark their way through life. If you believe that you have this kind of personality and that it is interfering with your quest for a degree, pick up a copy of Friedman and Ulmer's (1984) book *Treating Type A Behavior—and Your Heart* and follow their suggestions for learning to conduct yourself more like a milder-mannered "Type B." Type A behavior can be treated effectively without reducing your productivity.

Another kind of destructive overcommitment is unrealistic perfectionism. Some students do not finish their dissertations because they can never bring themselves to stop collecting information and start organizing it. Others falter because they are never satisfied with what they have written. Nothing, dissertations included, is ever perfect; for these people, this means that nothing is ever finished. Eileen, in our opening case histories, is an example of an unrealistic perfectionist.

Often students seek unattainable perfection because they are afraid to face the day when others will judge their work. If this is your problem, you need to learn how to let go. Like a parent with a growing child, you must allow the product of your efforts to stand forth and be evaluated on its merits.

Lack of Positive Feedback and Reinforcement. Home on the range may be the place where "never is heard a discouraging word," but many graduate students come to feel that their experience is just the opposite. To be sure, all graduate students, especially those writing a thesis or dissertation, must expect and be prepared to handle criticism. You are likely to be required to do several drafts of your paper. Because dissertation directors usually feel that their main job is to improve the dissertation, your director may bring mistakes to your attention while forgetting to mention the things you have done properly. On some days, you may be criticized simply because your director is out of sorts.

You must expect to roll with (and learn from) a certain number of punches—but no one should have to endure unrelieved gloom. If your director is too stingy with praise, ask him or her to point out the sections of your paper that you have done well. This will help you feel better about your proposal or dissertation and keep you from redoing sections that need no further improvement. Don't feel embarrassed to ask for the encouragement you need.

Another helpful, but somewhat more time-consuming, means for obtaining useful and supportive feedback is to arrange for consultation and review by your peers. Other students are likely to offer a good blend of expert advice and empathy, two very important items in helping you complete your dissertation. Consult with them about your writing, the content of your project, and your statistical analyses.

One good way of establishing peer review and consultation is to start a dissertation support group. It's advisable to recruit all group members from the same general field. They need not be from the same department, but they should usually be from the same discipline. While a great need exists for research that collaborates across disciplines, even long-term professionals often find such collaboration difficult. As a novice to research, you may find that cross-discipline collaboration simply confuses you.

Control the size of the group. The group should be large enough to allow for sufficient diversity but not so large that you cannot get its members together for regular meetings or that its meetings become unwieldy. Five reliable members is probably a good number.

Meet regularly, and obtain a commitment for regular attendance from each member. Make certain that no one member carries the burden for arranging all the meetings or providing the meeting places.

Make certain that early in each meeting or some time in advance, if possible, all members are provided with copies of any written materials to be discussed. Such materials include both dissertation abstracts and clearly written outlines of specific problems that are being encountered. Members should recognize that anything causing a problem for one of them will likely cause problems for all sooner or later and so should not be hesitant to suggest that the group discuss it.

Do not let meetings degenerate into mere gripe sessions, but be prepared to be supportive when a personal problem arises. Celebrate each member's successes, too. Shared successes are great motivators.

In addition to academic peers, make use of friends, relatives, and spouses as sources of feedback and support. These people usually care about you a great deal. Solicit special help from your spouse if you are married. Remember that he or she has a great deal of personal investment in your career and much to gain if you finish your dissertation. You may find that he or she wants to be more involved in your work, even though you are feeling guilty for having asked so much already.

You may need other reinforcers as well, since few rewards are built into the dissertation process. Most students are excited when their proposal is approved, but there is seldom a similar thrill before the successful final defense.

To offset this lack of reinforcement, plan intermediate reinforcers for yourself. One source of reinforcement can be a record of the work you have accomplished. If you have established a daily, weekly, or monthly goal for yourself, your record book itself can serve as a motivation. In addition, treat yourself to a reward when you reach an intermediate goal. Some students plan a special weekend excursion or buy a desired luxury as a reward for meeting a goal. Other students arrange to get out of a chore they dislike if their daily work is completed. One student agreed with his wife that he would do the dishes every night on which he had not met the work goal he had established for himself. "I was either going to finish my study or get dishpan hands," he laughed.

A third method is to tell others of your goals. Knowing that other people share your expectations can increase your motivation to accomplish what you set out to do.

Lack of Professional Skills

Lack of Planning Ability. By the time they reach graduate school, most students are used to leading extremely structured lives. Some have come to depend on external structure as a substitute for self-discipline. However, there are seldom any externally imposed schedules, quotas, or supervision during the writing of a dissertation. Students who have not learned to work independently, therefore, may find dissertation writing a frustrating experience. They discover that they are unable to organize their ideas, time, and resources effectively.

If lack of structure causes problems for you, you could ask your adviser to impose the external structure and schedules you need. However, this short-term solution does not address the underlying problem. A workshop in time or project management might provide useful tips on ways to organize your time and work efforts. You may also find the following approach helpful.

In order to plan how to use your time more effectively, you must first find out how you use it now. Take three or four days to explore how you really spend your time; you may make discoveries that surprise you. Divide your day into three periods: waking until lunch, lunch until dinner, and dinner until bedtime. Carry a notebook with you, and at the end of each period record every activity you did during that period and the amount of time the activity took. At the end of several days of recording, categorize the activities in your log and find the average daily time you spent on each. Order your categories from the most to the least time-consuming to get a rough picture of your current priorities.

Next, determine what goals are most important to you. Make a list of your long-range goals; then list reasonable one-year goals and goals for the coming month. Rank-order the items in each list according to their importance. Which are essential? Which are desirable but can be put off for a while? Which can be put off indefinitely because they don't really matter?

Break down the paths to your most important long- and intermediate-range goals into steps that can be accomplished in shorter periods of time. Combine the first step toward each of these goals with the most important of the goals already on your "this month" list. The six or eight highest-priority items in this combined list will become your major tasks for the month.

Finally, compare your current use of time with the priorities and goals you have established for yourself. Are you distributing your time in the way that will most effectively help you achieve your goals? If not, determine which activities should be given more of your time and which might get by with less.

For example, suppose your time log shows that you spend an average of three hours a day counseling friends. You find this activity rewarding and pleasurable, but you realize that it is distracting you from your long-range goal of completing your dissertation. You might decide to reduce the time you spend in counseling and devote those hours to writing instead.

By rank-ordering your priorities list and comparing it with your current-use-of-time log, you should arrive at a time-management agenda that allows you to continue normal living and still make progress toward completing your dissertation. Reassess your list each month. Some items on it will remain; others will drop off. Always break down the path to your goals into specific, easy-to-accomplish steps. Try to achieve one step toward your goal, no matter how small, each day.

Schedule one or more regular periods for work every day. Choose times when your mind is fresh and you can be alone and relatively free from distractions. Allow time for both focused and nonfocused thinking as well as for writing. Focused thinking allows you to study the major problem facing you that day and look for solutions to it. During nonfocused thinking, your mind should tune in to whatever emerges. This gives your unconscious mind an opportunity to feed your consciousness. Planned solitude provides an opportunity to confer with yourself and profit from your own creative ability.

Once you have worked out a realistic schedule, stick to it. Allow time for interruptions, unforeseen problems, and unscheduled events, but avoid permitting low-priority tasks to distract you frequently from more important goals. If you find yourself working on too many low-priority tasks, you may need to learn to say no—to yourself and to others. Reduce or eliminate unnecessary activities and commitments whenever possible. As much as you can, assign activities unrelated to your dissertation to the less productive periods in your day.

Set aside a regular and appropriate place as well as a regular time for uninterrupted work. Since academic work is associated with concentration, your work place should be as free from distraction as possible. A basement room in your home or a spare bedroom set up as an office might be a good choice. Many universities provide locked carrels for students engaged in thesis or dissertation research, and you might find that this sort of enclosure is perfect for you.

Lack of Technical Skills. Sometimes, because of poor advice, lack of personal commitment, or lapse of time between different parts of their studies, students find that they lack certain skills that they need for doing a dissertation. For example, at the time Karen began her graduate program in marriage and family therapy, her field required only a knowledge of descriptive statistics. Six years later, however, when she returned to her studies after her daughter started school, the field had become so complex that Karen could not do the necessary field-based research for her dissertation without a good knowledge of multivariate analysis. She had to take additional courses in statistics to fill in her "knowledge gap."

If you lack a necessary technical skill or body of knowledge, acquire it in the most efficient way possible. For example, if your study demands that you understand how to interpret the psychodiagnostic test developed by Hermann Rorschach, you will probably find that it makes more sense to attend a three-day clinic on Rorschach test interpretation than to enroll in a one-semester course on psychodiagnostics. On the one hand, don't waste time trying to become an expert in everything; on the other, don't neglect to provide yourself with all the skills you need. It's never a good idea to depend on someone else to provide a skill necessary for your dissertation.

Lack of Professional Contacts. Failing to develop and maintain professional contacts can prevent you from gaining access to experimental populations or knowing about people in your area who are doing work similar to yours. To keep this from happening, become acquainted with professionals in your general area of interest. Initiating contacts with experts is not as difficult as it may seem; many are eager to talk about their work.

One good way to develop contacts is to participate in professional organizations in your special field. If you are unsure which organizations to join, ask your adviser. Most professional organizations provide for student memberships. It's especially useful to become involved with the local chapters of these organizations. Attending local meetings provides a fine opportunity to interact with the organization's members.

Once you have attended meetings for a while, submit proposals for presentations at local professional gatherings. The exercise of preparing written material and then giving oral presentations is excellent for developing your professional abilities. It is also a way to become known, to tell the world that you believe you have something of value to contribute to your field. Such activity may lead to future job offers.

Make community contacts, too. The cooperation of the local community is necessary for many research projects. Education students, for example, frequently need the cooperation of local school personnel. Psychology students often must gain permission to conduct their research in community mental health settings or in industry. Social work students or political scientists may need help from government employees.

If you are in a program that requires a practicum or internship, you have a built-in way to develop some community contacts. If your program does not require field work, volunteer in an agency that you think might be helpful to you. Whatever your plan, begin developing contacts with appropriate representatives of the community early in your graduate career if you intend to conduct field research. This can increase your chances of gaining cooperation and help to avoid delays when your study actually begins.

Lack of Writing Skills. Failure to develop proper writing skills can delay completion of a dissertation or thesis and can produce a poor reception when it is finally submitted. Committee members often—and often correctly—see clumsy writing as a sign of sloppy thinking.

The best way to improve your writing skills is to write. To begin with, the discipline required to make your thoughts intelligible on paper helps to clarify your thinking. When you attempt to write about a subject, you may find that your knowledge of part of it is inadequate, for example. The question, "What am I really trying to say?" leads to the related questions, "What do I know about this?" and "What are my thoughts and attitudes about it?" You can clarify your purpose in writing only by first thinking through your material and then outlining each part of your message on paper.

When you gather research information, you accumulate isolated facts. They are then combined according to your interpretation and classification. As you group your facts, they develop into generalizations that will finally be written as a paragraph or section explaining a single topic or idea.

When you write, however, you need to organize your information in just the opposite order: Begin with the main theme and generalizations and then move toward illustrations, explanations, and details. These general guidelines may help you perfect this form of organization:

- Define unfamiliar terms before using them.
- Identify a table or diagram before interpreting it.
- Explain a general principle before applying it.
- Present a simple concept before a complex one.

Most institutions prefer a scientific or technical style to a literary or journalistic style for the writing of dissertations. A technical writing style accurately presents facts and systematized knowledge in a straightforward manner, appeals to reason, tends to use impersonal or technical language, shows a systematic or logical succession of ideas, and generally excludes unsupported opinions.

Don't let this style of writing put you in a literary straitjacket, however. By the time you begin to write your dissertation, you probably will have read and written enough papers to be familiar with the technical style of writing and its basic ground rules. A desire to adhere to the "accepted style" should never overshadow the fundamental rule of writing: be yourself.

Most authors occasionally need to refresh their memories on spelling, grammar, and the correct use of words. Be sure, therefore, to have the proper reference works on hand. These include a good dictionary and a good grammar book. Some of the best of the latter are Fowler's *Dictionary of Modern English Usage* (1965), Partridge's *Concise Usage and Abusage* (1954), and Perrin's *Writer's Guide and Index to English* (1978). You will find *Roget's International Thesaurus* (1977) a helpful book on synonyms.

You will probably also need to consult one or more style manuals at some point in your writing. For one thing, many universities recommend or even require writers of dissertations submitted to them to follow a particular style manual's format for such things as headings and subheadings, tables and figures, references cited in text, footnotes, quotations, references and bibliography, punctuation, spelling, capitalization, and use of italics. Before you begin to write your dissertation, find out what requirements of this kind, if any, apply to you.

Whether or not it is required, a style manual can be a great help if you have trouble expressing your ideas clearly in writing. For general style advice, read the brief but highly regarded *Elements of Style* by Strunk and White (1979). Other style manuals likely to be especially useful in preparing a dissertation include the *Publication Manual* of the American Psychological Association (American Psychological Association, 1983); *Form and Style: Theses, Reports, Term Papers* (Campbell, Ballou, and Slade, 1982); *A Manual of Style* (University of Chicago, 1982); and *A Manual for Writers of Term Papers, Theses, and Dissertations* (Turabian, 1973). Additional style manuals are listed in Appendix C. If your director has no preference, choose the manual required by or most compatible with the journals of your discipline.

Whenever possible, have your written work edited or critiqued. Papers done for courses offer some opportunity for this, but, unfortunately, professors often do not do a thorough job of critiquing writing style when grading course papers. Ask your professors to comment on the writing style as well as the content of your papers. When writing your dissertation or thesis, try to have a trusted person edit what you have written once a week or so. You may even wish to hire an editor, as described in Chapter Eight.

Finally, try to have some of your preliminary work published while you are working on your dissertation or thesis. Consider writing concept papers, literature reviews, or research articles associated with your subject. Having some of your early work published will bolster your confidence, enhance your future marketability, and provide valuable practice in carrying out and communicating research. The editorial process of most professional journals will help refine the research and writing skills you need to produce a quality dissertation. Don't let the production of other material take too much time away from your dissertation or thesis, however.

Any effort you spend to improve your ability to communicate ideas clearly and simply in writing will pay lifelong dividends. The scholars who are most cited and best remembered are almost always those who not only have something important to say but who say it in a precise, appealing, and memorable way.

Summary

Most graduate programs teach the skills needed, provide professional advice, and allow sufficient time for students to complete a degree. When students fail to gain their degrees or complete their theses or dissertations, the fault usually lies either in external obstacles or in defects in the students' attitudes or professional skills. This chapter described some common obstacles in each of these categories and suggested ways of overcoming them.

External problems faced by graduate students include financial hardship, conflict between study and job, and family problems. Financial hardship can be overcome by seeking student loans, on-campus jobs, or research grants. Careful planning of time and discussions with an employer can often solve conflicts between study and job. Family problems may require reallocation of time or, in serious cases, family counseling.

Excuses, lack of commitment, excessive commitment, and lack of positive feedback and reinforcement are common problems related to student attitude. A tendency to make excuses can be overcome by examining the excuses and trying to detect the real feelings and choices they disguise. A serious but not obsessive or perfectionist attitude provides a happy medium between lack of commitment and excessive commitment. Students can make up for a lack of positive feedback and reinforcement by asking advisers for positive comments, setting up groups for peer review, calling on friends and relatives for support, and planning their own intermediate reinforcers during the dissertation process.

A third kind of obstacle involves lack of professional or study skills. Skills that may be missing include planning ability, technical skills, professional contacts, and writing skills. Students can learn to organize their time by finding out how they currently spend their time and comparing this use of time to an ideal pattern of use based on a list of task priorities. They can make up for lack of technical skills by taking remedial courses. Lack of professional contacts can be remedied by joining professional organizations and making community contacts. The best way to correct a lack of writing skill is to write and have the result critiqued.

Chapter Two presents guidelines for selecting and developing a dissertation topic. It recommends a problem-oriented approach to this task and suggests that students begin their search for a topic early in their graduate program.

 TWO

Defining and Developing a Topic

Joanne began her search for a dissertation topic by reviewing the literature on the characteristics of instructional materials that aid learning. She soon developed an interest in Ausubel's (1960) concept of advance organizers and began to read extensively about research with organizers. Because she planned to become a teacher of mathematics or statistics, Joanne noted particularly those studies that concerned the learning of quantitative material. She found that most of the studies had used advance organizers in verbal form; few had tried a graphic or visual form, and most of those few had methodological problems. She decided, therefore, to concentrate her research on examining the effectiveness of visual organizers in teaching quantitative material. Her particular topic became the comparison of the effects of visual and verbal advance organizers on the learning of a unit in statistics.

Walter used a different approach to topic selection. While still taking courses, he became intrigued by canonical correlational analysis, the multivariate statistical procedure that examines the relationship between two sets of variables. He decided to use this technique in his dissertation, and he began to do a literature review on canonical analysis. He found many studies dealing with methodological issues involving canonical analysis, but he did not really want to do a methodological study. He found other studies that used the technique, but the content and focus of these studies was so varied that he quickly became confused and discouraged. Six months later, after switching to a problem-oriented approach to topic selection, Walter successfully defended a proposal for a study concerning the design of training materials—a study in which canonical correlational analysis played no part at all.

Selecting and developing a research topic can be the most important, difficult, time-consuming, and anxiety-producing parts of preparing a dissertation. When you select a research topic, you begin to construct the blueprint that will provide the structure for your entire study. As you develop the topic, you identify specific researchable problems and eventually focus on one of them. Drawing on a detailed literature search, you formulate the specific questions you will try to answer, the assumptions and theoretical framework that provide the context for those questions, the hypotheses you will test, and the methods by which you will test them.

Topic selection requires a substantial investment of time. Therefore, begin searching for a good dissertation or thesis topic while you are still taking graduate courses. Allow sufficient time to gather, analyze, and synthesize the information you need to define a specific problem.

Students generally are overly concerned with data collection or data analysis and consequently may fail to give adequate consideration to topic selection and development. Topic selection is difficult because it requires you to understand thoroughly a body of related information. A researchable topic usually emerges only after you have carefully analyzed and synthesized this information.

Many students fear that they will spend time exploring a topic and then will not be able to find a suitable problem to study. This fear generally is unfounded. After completing a review of literature on a particular subject, you are almost sure to be able to identify several researchable problems. Your biggest difficulty is likely to be in deciding which of these topics you want to explore in your dissertation.

Topic development can also produce considerable anxiety. Perhaps for the first time in your graduate program, you will be faced with accepting full control of what happens. An externally imposed schedule no longer controls you, and you have no immediate deadlines except those you impose on yourself. No end to your work will be in sight until you formulate your study well enough to be able to project an ending.

Selecting a Topic

Topic selection involves progression from a broad area of inquiry to specific problems within this area. You cannot make this progression without understanding the available literature. To select a topic suitable for a dissertation, you must be familiar with the state of the research in the area that you are considering. You must know what has been accomplished in the area, what hypotheses have or have not been supported, what the controversies are, what the unresolved issues are, what theories are applicable, and what contributions to theory have resulted from research. Your analysis, synthesis, and evaluation of the literature will help you select the topic on which you wish to work.

The process of topic selection normally develops something like this. Initially, you approach the literature with one or several ideas that might lead to topics. Each idea is associated with an area of inquiry that interests you. After exploring the literature in each area, you choose the area to which you think you can make the greatest contribution. You then embark on a comprehensive review of the literature concerning that area.

Your comprehensive review should enable you to identify several problems, any one of which could become a topic for your study. It should also point out relevant materials that will form the foundation for the development of your topic. Topic selection is complete when you choose a specific problem to study.

Approaches to Topic Selection. Students most commonly use one of three approaches when searching for a suitable topic. The approaches are problem oriented (emphasis on the problem itself), process oriented (emphasis on technique), and expediency oriented (emphasis on convenience). Of these three approaches, the problem-oriented one is by far the most likely to lead to discovery of a suitable topic in a reasonable amount of time. Most students who start with the process or expediency approaches succeed in finding a topic only after they switch to the problem-oriented approach. To see why, let's look at the differences in these three approaches.

A student who uses the problem-oriented approach simultaneously searches for a specific problem and the support necessary to provide the context for the study, evidence for its significance, and justification for its hypotheses. Ordinarily, this approach begins with an interest or a question and then moves into the literature. Once a specific topic is selected and support for it is developed, the design of the study usually follows logically and immediately. Joanne, in our opening example, used a problem-oriented approach.

A student who uses a process-oriented approach, by contrast, focuses on a specific instrument, a favorite treatment, or a special analytic strategy and then seeks to locate a researchable problem to which that process can be applied. In this approach, topic selection and problem definition become contingent on some other element. The range of possible topics is limited because of a prior choice. This is what happened to our other example student, Walter.

The problem with this approach is that its decision-making process is backward. Decisions about the process should follow decisions about the topic and the problem or at least should be made simultaneously. This approach may eventually lead to a researchable topic, but it is very inefficient and carries with it the danger that you will not be able to find a suitable problem because you will overlook topics in which you cannot use your favorite instrument or analytic strategy. Alternatively, you may settle on a topic, not because you are interested in it or find it significant, but because your instrument or analytic strategy is appropriate for it.

A student who uses the expediency-oriented approach selects a topic primarily on the basis of some preexisting condition. Such a student might seek a topic related to, for example, an existing or easily available data base, the student's current employment, or the interests of an adviser or someone else important to the student. The student might say, "I have these data; now let me look for a meaningful problem to which the data can be applied" or "Can I get a dissertation out of this project that I have to do for work?" or "My committee wants me to do this study. I guess I will, even though I am not very interested in it. With the support of my committee, I will be able to finish the study quickly."

Of course, if you are able to relate your study to an existing data base, your place of employment, or the interests of others, by all means do so. The point is simply that these should not be your first considerations in topic selection.

For example, a graduate student named Linda was successful in relating her dissertation topic to her employment. Linda worked for the U.S. Department of Defense training people who interpreted aerial photographs. She wanted to determine whether coloring small images in black-and-white photographs made the images easier to identify, a question with which she was directly involved at work. After a careful review of the literature, Linda developed an acceptable dissertation topic that involved a computer simulation of a figure identification task using both monochrome and color graphic displays. Linda's success came because she went beyond the convenience of drawing on her work, conceptualized a problem, and provided a rationale and supporting evidence that were firmly grounded in the literature. Thus, in the end, she used a problem-oriented rather than an expediency-oriented approach.

By contrast, Mary Lou became intrigued by the availability of a large data base and decided to do her dissertation on some topic that could be related to that data base. She experienced months of frustration because she could not develop an acceptable rationale for any topic she chose. The research questions she produced were trivial and not adequate for a dissertation. She was so captivated by the potential of the data base to support varied topics that she was unable to choose one of them and commit herself to an adequate exploration of it. Only when she went beyond the data base to investigate several topics thoroughly did she find an acceptable topic.

Aspects of all three approaches to topic selection can and often should be combined. Process and convenience can be important and useful factors to consider when choosing a topic; however, your main focus should always be on the problem itself. You must be sure that you will be able to conduct the research necessary to answer your questions, which means that you must consider carefully the methodology you will employ, your ability to obtain the data, and the amount of time you will need to conduct the research. These factors will be discussed later in this chapter.

How and Where to Look. Before you begin looking for a topic, consider the general kinds of things that interest you. For example, are you more interested in a topic that requires extensive field study or clinical experiments, or would you prefer one that involves historical methods? Would you like to use children, college students, or older adults in your study? Would you enjoy doing a purely methodological study, or would you rather do one that concerns, say, an application of learning theory, personality theory, or social networks? Note that these questions need not lead to a process-oriented approach, since they do not focus on specific methods.

Begin with a general idea of the type of topic that appeals to you, but don't be too narrow at first. Narrowing your search too soon may cause you to overlook promising aspects of a topic. Once you find a topic area that appeals to you, however, learn all you can about it. The knowledge you gain may well prove useful even if you decide not to do your research on that topic.

Whenever you search for a potential topic, take notes. These will become your personal storehouse of information. Without a good note-taking system, you run the risk of having to retrieve material again or of losing it forever.

The logical place to begin your topic search is with your graduate experience. As you progress through your courses, particularly the seminars, look for potential topics for your dissertation. When you come upon an area that interests you, learn more about it by doing reading beyond the course requirements or by using independent study or directed readings courses. Beginning your topic search while you are still taking courses often means that by the time your courses are finished, your topic selection is finished as well. Students who are ready to begin their dissertation research soon after completing their course program tend to finish their degrees faster and do more significant studies than those who wait until they have taken their last course before they begin to explore potential dissertation topics.

The following examples show how two students used their graduate programs to the fullest in searching for topics. Paul was a college physical education instructor before entering his doctoral program. He enrolled in a program in measurement and evaluation because of his interest in the reliability of measures used in the context of physical education, such as judges' ratings for diving, gymnastics, and figure skating. Throughout his doctoral program, Paul read extensively about reliability theory and its applications. All the while he was carefully planning his doctoral research. A short time after he had passed his comprehensive examinations, Paul presented his proposal, and within a few months he completed his dissertation.

Paul was exceptional; very few graduate students plan their research from the very beginning of their doctoral program. Larry was more typical. He became interested in his topic as a result of readings he did while preparing for an advanced seminar in anthropology. Larry continued to refine his ideas during the seminar, and by the time the seminar was over, he was well on the way to developing his proposal. As Paul had done, Larry presented his proposal shortly after passing his comprehensive examinations. Six months later he successfully defended his dissertation.

A second source for topics is the current research interests and activities of the professors in your program. If you select a topic that falls into this category, you have the advantage of immediate access to practicing researchers. When you and a professor develop an interest in the same topic, you may become part of a team rather than just another student on whose committee the professor happens to serve.

Reading journals germane to your discipline will help you keep abreast of progress in your field and enable you to explore potential research topics at the same time. Pay particular attention to books and periodicals that publish review articles, such as the *Review of Educational Research, Sociological Review,* the *Annual Review of Psychology,* and the *Review of Research in Education.* A review article not only helps you learn of developments in your field but also provides you with a rather extensive bibliography that can form the basis for a complete review of literature once you find a likely topic. Also, the authors of review articles usually indicate what further work needs to be done in the area. Their recommendations can give you useful guidance.

A fourth source for topics is unpublished research presented at professional meetings. By attending professional meetings regularly during your graduate program, you can hear presentations of current research, immediately obtain copies of papers presented, and interact directly with the researchers.

You can also look for unpublished research by using a retrieval system such as ERIC (Educational Resources Information Center). However, it is usually unwise to do retrieval system searches when you are just beginning to look for a topic. These searches are only as good as the input you give them. Searches made before you have focused your topic area can be expensive, time-consuming, and unproductive. Even after you have identified a potential topic, do as much of your own library work as possible before turning to the retrieval system. Computerized retrieval searches are discussed in more detail in Chapter Three.

Other dissertations are still another fruitful hunting ground for topics. Examine the titles of dissertations by graduates of your program as well as titles published in *Dissertation Abstracts International.* If a title appeals to you, read the abstract of the study. If you are still interested, get a copy of the document and read especially the literature review and the suggestions for further research.

Criteria for Topic Selection. A topic appropriate for a dissertation should satisfy at least six criteria, three related to the topic itself and three involving your interaction with it. An appropriate topic should be:

- sufficiently delimited
- significant
- unique
- interesting to you
- appropriate to your background
- feasible in terms of time, ability, and support

Let's look in more detail at these criteria to see what they mean and why they are so important.

First, you need to narrow or *delimit* your topic enough to make the purpose of your research clear to yourself and others. Sufficient delimitation helps you organize your literature search and produce a specific problem statement with accompanying theoretical rationale. In the first example presented in this chapter, Joanne narrowed her topic to the use of visual advance organizers with quantitative material. By the time she reached that point, she had also identified most aspects of the theoretical rationale for her topic.

A sufficiently delimited topic also helps your director and committee evaluate its appropriateness. General topics, such as "learning strategies," "administrative styles," "counseling theories," or "family networks" will probably evoke a rather noncommittal response. Your director cannot provide useful advice until you decide exactly what you wish to study.

A study on a *significant* topic makes a useful contribution to its field. While the ultimate judges of the significance of your study are the members of your committee, you must present arguments for its significance based on the literature. There are at least two types of significance to consider. The first is theoretical significance, the contribution you will make by adding new knowledge to the field. Theoretical significance is a requirement for all doctoral dissertations. The second is practical significance, the importance of the application of the study results to specific situations. You should develop arguments for both types of significance.

Research for a doctoral dissertation must be original work on a *unique* topic that adds new knowledge to the literature. Most master's theses also make original contributions. You must be sure, therefore, that your research is original, and you must convince others that it is so. One purpose of your comprehensive review of the literature is to determine whether what you want to study has been done before. Don't worry unduly about not being able to find a unique topic, however. With the knowledge explosion that continues to occur in all disciplines, it is relatively easy to design a study in a way that will make it an original contribution.

Production of a dissertation is a challenging task that requires many skills and abilities, most of all perseverance. You must have great *interest* in your research problem in order to cope with the frustrations and obstacles you are sure to encounter. It is hard enough to sustain enthusiasm and enjoyment over the term of a study if you are totally fascinated by your topic; it is practically impossible if you aren't.

Selecting a topic *appropriate* to your training has several advantages. First, you will save time, if only because you will be dealing with a familiar literature base. Second, you will be able to think and talk about your topic easily. Third, you are likely to receive more support from your professors for a topic about which you have some knowledge.

In addition, selecting a topic that matches your most developed skills reduces concern that you will lack the technical background required for your study. It is usually unwise to select a topic that demands a level of technical expertise you do not possess. If you greatly desire to investigate a topic that requires such a level of skill, plan additional work time to acquire the new skills before you begin writing your proposal.

Determine whether your topic is *feasible* for you to work on. To begin with, do you have the time that this topic will demand? Even a part-time job limits the time you have free for dissertation work, a factor you should consider when selecting your topic. If you work full time, it is practical to choose a study that can be conducted during evenings, weekends, holidays, and vacations.

Will you be able to obtain the data you need? When you begin to plan your study, consider the type of data it will require and some potential data sources so that you won't design yourself into a corner. Think about what assistance may be required from others and how likely you are to receive this assistance. Such assistance may consist of help in collecting data, conducting experiments, obtaining permission needed to gain access to subjects, or identifying cooperative subjects. If you plan to use an existing data base, you will need to know how to obtain it or gain access to it, how much it will cost, and how to use it when you receive it. You can usually find help in resolving technical problems involved in reading or manipulating the data from data bases, however.

Do you have adequate support for your study? Your director and committee make up one vital source of support. Choose a committee that can and will actively assist you, then draw freely on their expertise. (Don't act helpless, however; remember that *you* must take the most active role in your study.)

Make certain that you will also have access to any technical assistance that your study requires. You may need help in scoring and coding, for example. Make certain you have access to a computer for processing and analyzing data. Assure yourself that the necessary software is available, and learn how to use it or where to find help in using it. Chapter Eight provides more information on computers and technical assistance.

Developing the Topic

Once you select your topic and decide on a problem to investigate, you need to develop the topic so that you can:

- write a specific problem statement;
- construct a theoretical framework for your study;
- formulate research questions and hypotheses; and
- identify the assumptions on which the study will be based.

Problem Analysis. As you searched for potential topics, your review of the literature was at first general and then began to center on a particular topic. Now that you have identified the specific problem on which you wish to concentrate, focus your review precisely on that problem so that you can identify what is known, not known, and conjectured about it; what variables relate to it, their relative importance, and the functional relationships that exist among them; and what needs to be known about the problem and what is feasible to research.

After you have collected the known and suspected facts about your problem, you need to sift through all the evidence and suggest possible explanations for those facts. Like topic selection, problem analysis takes time and careful thought. It will involve both inductive and deductive reasoning.

In inductive reasoning, you observe particular instances of some phenomenon and then make a general conclusion about the phenomenon; in other words, you start with specific observations and combine them to produce a more general statement of relationship. In conducting research, most often you are able to examine only some instances of a phenomenon. Using this imperfect induction, you arrive at conclusions with a certain degree of probability. When you evaluate particular research studies and arrive at a generalization concerning them, you are using inductive reasoning. For example, a generalization that the presence of certain syntactic structures, such as passive voice or if-then conditional statements, inhibits the comprehension of written materials by hearing-impaired individuals follows by induction from a series of research studies demonstrating that removing those structures from written materials improves the performance of hearing-impaired subjects.

Deductive reasoning, by contrast, goes from the general to the specific; you argue for the truth of a conclusion based on the truth of some premise. Usually this is done in the form of a syllogism. A syllogism consists of three propositions: the major premise, the minor premise, and the conclusion. A common type of syllogism that occurs in research studies is: If A, then B (major premise); A happens (minor premise); therefore B follows (conclusion). The validity of the conclusion of a deductive argument depends on the truth of the premises and the proper relationship of the minor premise to the conclusion. You use deductive reasoning when you base your major premise on some established theory and argue for the conclusion after assuming the minor premise is true.

The following example shows how deductive reasoning might be used in a problem analysis. In a study based on the instructional theory of Gagne (1977), a student named Philip argued as follows:

> If prerequisite internal conditions are present in the learner and if the appropriate external conditions are arranged, then the desired learning will occur (major premise). The presence of internal conditions is assumed, and the external conditions will be arranged (minor premise). Desired learning will then occur (conclusion).

In designing his research, Philip assumed that the students who would participate in the study possessed the necessary intellectual skills (internal conditions) to learn the instructional material that would be presented. He then randomly assigned the students to one of two classes, in each of which a different teaching strategy was used to present identical material (external conditions). After an extended instructional period, the students in one of the classes performed better on a test sampling the material than did the students in the other class. Philip then argued (inductively) that the one teaching strategy was superior to the other in facilitating the learning of the material. Philip used deductive reasoning to argue the reasonableness of his hypothesis; however, he used inductive reasoning to argue the truth of his conclusion—that the hypothesis was indeed correct.

Problem Statement. A problem statement is the concrete and explicit specification of the exact problem that you will study. It should include all the facts, relationships, and explanations that your analysis of the problem showed to be relevant. The problem statement follows your description of the context of the problem, which should contain enough background information to establish the setting of the problem; the major findings on which you are going to base your argument; and your argument, presented deductively if possible.

In the problem statement itself you state precisely what you intend to do in your study. Problems may be expressed either as questions (the most common form) or as statements. Your problem statement should make your research questions and hypotheses obvious, even though they may not yet be stated explicitly.

As you continue to review the literature, new information and additional insights may require you to reevaluate and revise your problem statement. When additional reading sheds no further light on the problem and when your insights converge and stabilize, you have delimited the problem sufficiently to finalize your statement.

Theoretical Framework. The theoretical framework of your study is the structure you impose on the information that you have collected about your problem. This framework provides the context of your study, its rationale, and its significance. The ingredients for your theoretical framework come from your analysis, synthesis, and evaluation of the literature plus your own insights into the problem. A theoretical framework typically consists of a discussion of:

- specific theories related to the problem;
- what is known about the problem from other empirical studies;
- important variables and how they relate to the problem;
- what needs to be done to advance knowledge concerning the problem; and
- specific populations of importance to the problem.

Figure 1 presents a theoretical framework for a study to determine the effect of modified test instruments on the relationship between personality variables and achievement in deaf adolescents. This framework is similar to that used by Koelle (1981) in his dissertation. The major dimensions of the framework are personality variables, achievement, and deaf populations. Self-concept and locus of control are the personality variables of interest. Koelle reviewed the literature for the theoretical foundations of each of these variables, specific empirical find-

Figure 1. Schematic Representation of a Theoretical Framework.

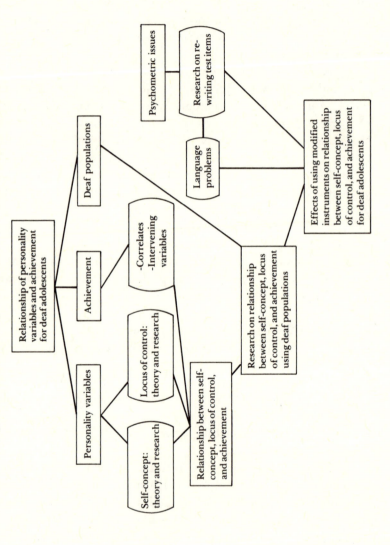

ings concerning each, and the relationship between these variables and achievement. He then reviewed the achievement literature for important correlates of achievement and necessary intervening variables. His review of the literature on deaf populations concentrated on specific findings relevant to self-concept, locus of control, and achievement. This review revealed that deaf people have difficulty understanding certain syntactic structures of written language. The specific problem he decided to examine in his study was the effect that modifying instruments containing difficult syntactic structures would have on the relationship between self-concept, locus of control, and achievement in deaf adolescents. This choice of problem required him to add a psychometric component to his framework.

Exhibit 1 presents another example of a theoretical framework, this time in the form of an outline of topics for the re-

Exhibit 1. Outline of a Review of Literature Chapter.

Introduction
Definition of Terms
Self-Esteem Theory and Historical Background
Social Role-Taking Ability
    Definition and Theory
    Stages According to Selman
    Method and Measurement According to Selman
    Developmental Findings
Self-Esteem and Social Role-Taking Ability
Self-Esteem and Parental Acceptance-Rejection
    Influence Due to Perceived Parental Difference
        Sex of Parents and Children
        Closeness and Harmony in the Parental Environment
    Influence Due to Chronological Age of the Child
Social Role-Taking Ability and Parental Acceptance-Rejection
Social Role-Taking Ability and Empathy
Other Factors Influencing the Development of Social Role-Taking Ability
Causal Model Relationships and Structure
Summary

---

view of literature section of a proposal developed by a graduate student for a study on some factors influencing the development of self-esteem in preadolescent children. The major components of the framework are self-esteem theory, social role-

taking ability, and parental acceptance-rejection. After presenting the theoretical foundations and empirical findings germane
to his study for both self-esteem and social role-taking ability,
the student related these to each other and each to parental
acceptance-rejection. Next, he reviewed the relationship between
social role-taking ability and empathy as well as other factors influencing social role-taking ability. Finally, he proposed a model
postulating a relationship among the major variables in the
study.

   In addition to providing a context for your study, your
theoretical framework should provide a context for the integra-
tion of your findings within a larger area of inquiry. Your review of literature chapter contains the complete documentation
of your theoretical framework. Ordinarily, you also summarize
this framework in the first chapter of your study to provide the
foundation for your problem statement.

   Questions and Hypotheses. As a result of your analysis of
the problem and the organization of your theoretical framework, you should formulate one or several major research questions that your study will address. To arrive at these major questions, write down as many related questions as you can as you
analyze your problem. Judge the significance of each question
and its relationship to your theoretical framework. Finally,
group related questions to form more general questions.

   Next, construct one or several hypotheses that provide
possible answers to the questions you have raised. You should
use both deductive and inductive reasoning to formulate your
hypotheses, drawing on relevant theory and previous research
findings. Your theoretical framework should provide some justification for each hypothesis. Your hypotheses will focus inquiry, determine relevant independent and dependent variables,
and provide the foundation for explaining the results of your research and arriving at appropriate conclusions. Note that the
first hypotheses that occur to you will not necessarily be the
best; higher quality hypotheses often result if you continue to
search for other plausible explanations after you have found
some that are compatible with your theoretical framework.
Some examples of hypotheses are given in Chapter Five.

Assumptions. The final step in developing your topic is identification of the assumptions underlying your study in general and your hypotheses in particular. Students often confuse hypotheses and assumptions. In research, hypotheses are assertions subject to verification, whereas assumptions are truths that are accepted without proof.

All studies have assumptions. You should identify the assumptions behind your study and examine them carefully. You may find that some of them are not plausible, in which case you should analyze your problem further. You will need to list the most critical of your assumptions in the first chapter of your proposal so that your readers can evaluate them and understand the foundations on which your theoretical framework and hypotheses rest. Some examples of assumptions are given in Chapter Five.

Summary

This chapter presented guidelines for selecting and developing an appropriate dissertation topic. It is wise to begin looking for a topic while you are still taking courses. Take a problem-oriented rather than a process-oriented or expediency-oriented approach to topic selection.

Begin with a broad subject area that interests you and, through appropriate readings and searches of the literature, narrow this area down to one or several specific topics that your study might investigate. Good sources of possible topics include your graduate courses, the current interests of your professors, journal articles, papers presented in professional meetings, material in on-line retrieval systems, and other dissertations.

The topic you finally choose should be sufficiently delimited, significant, and unique. It should also be interesting to you, appropriate to your background, and feasible in terms of your time, ability, and available support.

Development of a topic begins with analysis of the problem you have chosen, using both inductive and deductive reasoning. Use your analysis of the problem and the literature relevant to it to prepare a problem statement and theoretical framework

for your proposal. As you develop your topic, you will also formulate questions and hypotheses concerning it and identify the
assumptions that lie behind them. Your development phase will
synthesize the results of your literature search and all the other
research you have done up to this point, thereby preparing you
to write your proposal.

The next chapter describes how to use library personnel,
services, and reference materials to aid your literature search as
you identify and develop your topic.

 THREE

Making Effective Use
of Special Library Resources

Harry chose as his dissertation topic a comparison of traditional teaching methods and a program using the Logo computer language in increasing the artistic skills of fourth graders. He began a literature search on this topic by making the acquaintance of the librarians in both the Education and the Computer Sciences libraries in his university. His background was primarily in computer science, so he sometimes encountered terms related to education research that were unfamiliar to him. He looked these up in the *Dictionary of Education.*

As his literature search continued, Harry composed a bibliography of materials to read by consulting handbooks and review sources related to his field. He added other books and articles by consulting indexes and abstracting services such as *Child Development Abstracts and Bibliography.* He worked out an efficient strategy for computer searching of ERIC and other on-line data bases for articles related to his topic. He looked up several kinds of tests for measuring artistic ability. He soon completed a comprehensive literature search related to his topic.

The importance of the library to your academic and research success cannot be overestimated. The more comfortable you are with the facilities, personnel, services, and resources of libraries in your area, the greater the benefits you will derive from them.

Getting Acquainted

Most academic libraries offer orientation sessions throughout the year, including tours of library facilities and collections, bibliographic instruction classes, and library user seminars. Take advantage of these programs; you may learn about services and materials you never knew existed.

Regain your acquaintance with a library by making contact with the librarians. Many academic libraries are staffed by subject specialists who concentrate on building the library collection in specific disciplines. Identify the people in your home institution who are most familiar with your area of research and interest them in your topic. Ask them to help you find the sources you need to get started on your project. Share your successes and failures with them. Cultivating research allies in the library will have many long-term advantages.

Next, spend time browsing in the library reference collection. Notice *types* of reference materials in your area of interest. Look for dictionaries and encyclopedias that might help you narrow or broaden a topic and bibliographies of the literature in your area. Notice the existence of indexing and abstracting services, literature reviews, handbooks, directories, and bibliographic sources. For an overview of the reference sources available in your discipline, examine the entries in Eugene P. Sheehy's *Guide to Reference Books* (1976) and its supplements (1980 and 1982).

Identify library services that may be useful to you. For example, how much reference assistance can you receive by telephone? Often a quick call to the reference desk will produce a date, statistic, address, name, or referral that saves you hours of time.

Is your library part of a consortium or some other cooperative structure? Such arrangements can provide you with quick access to materials not available in your home library.

How can interlibrary loan services assist you? These services allow you to obtain materials from other libraries anywhere in the country at little or no cost. A member of your library staff will identify the institution owning the material you need and will order it for your use. You are required only to supply complete bibliographic information for the desired item. Allow at least two weeks for delivery of materials from an interlibrary loan.

Are computer search services available? If so, what is the scope of these services? They may provide access to a broad array of bibliographic data bases in the behavioral and social sciences, to more specific data bases, or both.

Has your library an on-line computer catalog for public access? If so, spend time refining your skill in searching by subjects, keywords, and other bibliographic elements. Computerized bibliographic catalogs provide many more access points than do traditional card or book catalogs, and so can be more useful. Be sure to inquire, however, whether all of the library's holdings are in the on-line catalog. Since the process of converting bibliographic files to machine-readable form is time consuming and expensive for libraries, older acquisitions often are not included in on-line catalogs. Therefore, you may have to continue to use the card or printed catalogs in addition to the computerized catalog.

Does your library have special files or indexes that may have been locally developed specifically for graduate students? Some libraries collect tests and measurement instruments, pamphlets, research reports, and other useful ephemeral material and organize them in special locations or files that are unknown to the casual library user. These collections usually are not listed in library catalogs and therefore are not easily identified unless a librarian points them out.

Are any special facilities available for graduate students? Can a private study carrel be reserved for your use? Are lockers available for secure storage of your files and notes? If these facilities exist, arrange for their use early in the semester. They can add greatly to your comfort and convenience.

Finally, be sure to gather and read through all the general-information brochures, flyers, schedules, and pertinent biblioggraphies produced by the library. They may save you a trip to a library closed for Founders Day, for example.

Reference Works

Encyclopedias and Dictionaries. A scholarly encyclopedia is a natural place to begin your background research. Such encylopedias usually contain easy-to-locate, well-rounded articles that present topics with major points logically arranged and accompanied by selected bibliographies. Among the standard titles available in most university collections are the *International Encyclopedia of the Social Sciences* (1968), the *Encyclopedia of Psychology* (Eysenck and Arnold, 1972), the *Encyclopedia of Education* (1971), the *International Encyclopedia of Higher Education* (1977), *The International Encyclopedia of Psychiatry, Psychology, Psychoanalysis, and Neurology* (1977), and the *Encyclopedia of Social Work* (1977).

When using encyclopedias, as with all reference sources, be aware of publication dates and the availability of supplementary volumes and indexes.

Familiarize yourself also with specialized dictionaries that define terms and concepts in your field. The *Dictionary of Behavioral Science* (Wolman, 1973), the *Dictionary of Education* (Good, 1973), *A Dictionary of the Social Sciences* (Gould and Kolb, 1964), and the *Psychology Almanac* (Wilkening, 1973) are a few of the titles available in most library reference collections. The *Acronyms, Initialisms, and Abbreviations Dictionary* (1983-1984) and its supplements will also prove invaluable as you encounter contractions and condensations in the literature.

Handbooks and Review Sources. Handbooks and review sources gather, digest, and relate many significant facts, methods, research findings, and developments that are scattered through periodicals, reports, and miscellaneous documents. In addition, a bibliographical essay in your area of interest can be a valuable discovery. Such an essay can fill in a good deal of relevant background for your topic or further limit, expand, or define it.

The following list shows some of the most useful and recent handbooks in the behavioral sciences. It is well worth perusing these volumes at the outset of your research project.

American Handbook of Psychiatry (Arieti, 1974)
Annual Review of Anthropology (annual)
Annual Review of Psychology (annual)
Carmichael's Manual of Child Psychology (Mussen, 1970)
Encyclopedia of Educational Research (1982)
Handbook of Abnormal Psychology (Eysenck, 1973)
Handbook of Applied Psychology (Fryer and Henry, 1950)
Handbook of Clinical Psychology (Wolman, 1965)
Handbook of Personality Theory and Research (Borgatta and Lambert, 1968)
Handbook of Psychotherapy and Behavior Change (Garfield and Bergin, 1978)
Handbook of Small Group Research (Hare, 1976)
Handbook of Social Psychology (Lindzey and Aronson, 1968-1970)
The Psychoanalytic Study of the Child (Annual)
Review of Child Development Research (1970-1975)
Review of Educational Research (quarterly)
Review of Research in Education (annual)
Third Handbook of Research on Teaching (Wittrock, in press).

Bibliographies. In addition to handbooks and review sources, bibliographies are published on almost every aspect of research. To locate such bibliographies, search for your topic in the library card catalog. Study the two-volume *Library of Congress Subject Headings* (1980) to determine the best subject heading to use. If you are interested in a bibliography on old age, for example, you would find the heading AGING—BIBLIOGRAPHY to be the most useful.

Another approach to locating a suitable bibliography is to consult the *Bibliographic Index: A Cumulative Bibliography of Bibliographies*. This reference tool, published annually and updated three times a year, includes separately published bibliographies, parts of books, or bibliographic articles in over 1,900 periodicals. The subject arrangement of this source makes it especially easy to use.

Indexes to Recent Books. To make your literature search complete and up to date, you must know about recently published materials in your field. Several sources are available for identifying such works. *Books in Print,* published annually, includes two volumes of a *Subject Guide to Books in Print.* By using the Library of Congress subject headings, you may be able to identify a recently published bibliography or other book on your topic that is as yet unavailable in your library. *Forthcoming Books,* which appears bimonthly, includes a subject section that can be used in the same manner. This book-finding tool supplements *Books in Print* and includes complete bibliographic information for books to be published within the next five months.

The *Cumulative Book Index,* published monthly and cumulating periodically, permits subject searching of books published in the English language anywhere in the world. Subjects are interfiled with authors and titles in one alphabetical listing. Prepublication announcements of books are not made, but this resource's international scope can make it especially helpful if your topic requires that type of coverage.

Other Indexes and Abstracting Services. When you review the literature in your topic area, you must search periodicals and other literature sources to enlarge and update your bibliography. Periodical indexes, abstracting services, and citation indexes can aid you in this task. The following are among the most useful references of this kind for education and the behavioral sciences.

Abstracts in Anthropology
    Since 1970 this quarterly publication has indexed and abstracted books, articles, and conference papers in ethnology, linguistics, and other aspects of anthropology. Author and subject indexes are cumulated annually.
Abstracts of Instructional and Research Materials in Vocational and Technical Education
    Covers agricultural, business, career, health, consumer,

home economics, trade, and industrial education. A special section announces "Projects in Progress," research funded through the U.S. Bureau of Occupational and Adult Education. This resource is published quarterly.

Child Development Abstracts and Bibliography

A quarterly publication that abstracts periodical articles on child development from biological, psychological, educational, medical, and other points of view. It also includes brief descriptive reviews of books dealing with child development. Published three times a year.

Education Index

Indexes periodicals, proceedings, yearbooks, monographs, bulletins, and some U.S. government publications in all areas of education, curriculum, administration, finance, counseling, and guidance. The "Book Review" section is especially useful. The index is issued monthly and cumulates annually.

Educational Administration Abstracts

A quarterly journal containing abstracts of articles from approximately eighty journals dealing with societal factors, values, economic development, and other topics that affect educational policies and programs.

Educational Resources Information Center (ERIC)

An information system that collects, indexes, and disseminates educational research information and material. (Education is interpreted very broadly, so many aspects of the behavioral sciences are included.) Documents in ERIC, most of which are available on microfiche as well as in hard copy, are indexed and abstracted in *Resources in Education* (RIE). Periodical articles can be identified through the indexing and abstracting in *Current Index to Journals in Education* (CIJE). Most libraries that subscribe to ERIC maintain files of the microfiche documents indexed in RIE.

Exceptional Child Education Resources

This service, issued quarterly, covers important publications in all aspects of special education for the handicapped or gifted. It includes research reports, journal articles, curriculum guides, texts, activity manuals, and non-print media.

Language and Language Behavior Abstracts (LLBA)
International in scope, LLBA deals with special education, speech and language, and verbal learning. It is issued quarterly with annual cumulated indexes.

Psychological Abstracts
Provides nonevaluative summaries and citations of periodical articles, dissertations, books, and unpublished documents. This monthly publication is the major abstracting service for psychology.

Public Affairs Information Service Bulletin (PAIS)
A weekly publication that indexes periodicals, pamphlets, books, speeches, government documents, and other authoritative materials relevant to education, economic and social conditions, public administration, and international relations.

Social Sciences Citation Index (SSCI)
Issued three times a year, SSCI contains cited references to journals, books, book reviews, theses, reports, proceedings of meetings, personal correspondence, internal communications, and papers awaiting publication. This tool is the most comprehensive indexing system in the social sciences. It may be difficult for the novice to use, but with a bit of assistance from a librarian, time spent using SSCI may prove very rewarding. This important index can also be searched on-line.

Social Sciences Index
Supersedes *Social Sciences and Humanities Index.* Includes periodical articles in the fields of anthropology, psychology, sociology, education, and related subjects. Issued quarterly with annual cumulations.

Social Work Research and Abstracts
Offers abstracts of articles and dissertations as well as five or six complete research papers in each issue. This quarterly publication supersedes *Abstracts for Social Workers,* which was published from 1965 to 1977. It covers service, social policy and action, service methods, and related fields of knowledge. The index is cumulated annually.

Sociological Abstracts
  Published six times a year, this service provides indexing
  and abstracting for very broad and nearly comprehensive
  coverage of all aspects of sociology. The abstracts are arranged by classification and include journal articles as well
  as conference papers. The index cumulates annually.
Dissertation Abstracts International (DAI)
  This monthly publication presents abstracts of doctoral
  dissertations accepted at many American universities and
  some European institutions as well. Complete dissertations
  are available on microfilm or in hard-copy reproduction
  from University Microfilms in Ann Arbor, Michigan. The
  abstracts are indexed in the *Comprehensive Dissertation
  Index,* a keyword index based on dissertation titles. Entries
  include full title, author, degree granted, date, university,
  number of pages, code for locating the abstract of the dissertation in DAI, and order number. Many students have
  found it useful to browse through the broad subject areas
  in their field of interest, using appropriate keywords to
  identify dissertations written on related aspects of their
  topics. Such dissertations may contain useful bibliographies, methodologies, measurement instruments, or suggestions for further research. *Dissertation Abstracts* may
  also be searched on-line.

Computer Searches

Printed reference books, bibliographic tools, information
sources, monographs, papers, reports, and journals are more and
more often being replaced by on-line data base services such as
those available through Lockheed (DIALOG), System Development Corporation (ORBIT), and Bibliographic Retrieval Services, Inc. (BRS). Most university libraries will have access to
these data bases. Some can also be accessed on microcomputers
through services such as The Source.

Several types of data bases especially relevant to the behavioral sciences can be accessed through libraries. *Sociological
Abstracts, Psychological Abstracts,* and ERIC are a few examples of bibliographic or "reference" data bases. There is also a

growing body of "source" data bases that include dictionary or handbook-type information, such as the *Foundation Directory* and the *Encyclopedia of Associations*. A third type is "numeric" data bases such as IMPRESS (Interdisciplinary Machine Processing for Research and Education in Social Sciences), which contain statistical data from numerous social science surveys, selected U.S. Census information, and elsewhere. Full text searching—that is, computer searching of keywords found in the text of a document—is available in a number of these data bases. Document delivery, or the production of an entire article, document, or report on- or off-line, is now also possible in many cases.

Many of the indexes and collections of abstracts listed in the previous section can be searched quickly and efficiently by computer. Bibliographic citations in computer files or data bases are given in the same form as that used in print. Most indexes have only relatively recent files available to computer searching, however. For example, *Psychological Abstracts,* which began publication in 1927, is available only from 1967 to date. (Note, however, that all of ERIC is available on line.) In most cases these time limitations will not be critical, but they could become a serious problem if you are doing a historical study.

Most computer data bases do not include many books or monographs, since they were established mainly as indexes to periodical articles, reports, documents, and dissertations. Two exceptions are Research Libraries Information Network (RLIN) and On-line College Library Center (OCLC). These two national data bases of ten to twenty million bibliographic records could prove useful to update and verify bibliographic citations. In addition to providing access by author and title, which both OCLC and RLIN permit, RLIN can be accessed by key words.

In academic libraries, computer search services are usually handled by librarians specially trained to communicate with the computer quickly, efficiently, and accurately. Since the cost of computer time makes up a large part of the expense of a search, you will want to use that time economically. Try to prepare an efficient search strategy before scheduling a search. If you plan to access a data base through your home computer and are not an experienced searcher, it would be wise to consult a librarian about efficient strategies before you begin searching.

The best strategy for retrieving information from a data base will depend in part on the type of indexing the data base uses—that is, whether the indexing uses keywords from titles only or keywords found in the text of the abstract or complete article as well. In the *Social Sciences Citation Index,* for example, each citation in an article is separately indexed.

The most important part of any search strategy is stating your research problem clearly. The more specific you are in presenting your problem, the more fruitful will be the results you obtain. Remember that the computer can search all years available and several aspects of your topic at the same time. Prepare a list of subject headings, keywords, and variant phrases that could possibly produce material on your topic and give this list to your librarian-searcher.

You should also have a good idea of what you do *not* want to include in your search. If you have done some searching in printed sources and wish to omit those sources from the computer search, tell your searcher. If you know which data bases you would like to have searched, indicate these, but allow the searcher to use his or her judgment and experience in determining which files to consult. The searcher may be able to eliminate redundant searches, thereby saving you time and money.

Often, as the searcher prepares the search strategy, you will be present to suggest a broadening or narrowing of the search's scope. You will know immediately how many citations on your topic can be produced at any point in the search. The purpose of your search—selecting, narrowing, broadening, exploring a topic, or identifying all supporting research for a narrow, well-defined topic—will dictate the number of citations you want or the years you wish to cover.

Once the search strategy is established, the librarian can request that the remainder of the search be printed "off-line," usually at a location outside the library, on a high-speed printer. Delivery of the complete search is made in about one week. The advantage of using this option is a lower printing and time charge, since such searches are run at hours when computer use is lower and computer time is therefore less expensive.

Investigate the availability of free data base searches for graduate students at your institution. Often there is a special fund to pay for graduate researchers' computer time.

Statistical Information and Test Instruments

Statistical Information. In addition to bibliographic information, computer searches can retrieve sources of statistical information that you may require in your research. The *American Statistics Index* (ASI), a comprehensive guide and index to the statistical publications of the U.S. government, is available online. This source is useful for identifying periodical articles, annuals, and biannuals on many aspects of education and the social and behavioral sciences. The ASI is published annually and supplemented monthly. Most university libraries subscribe to at least the printed index.

Additional sources of statistical information in education and the behavioral sciences can be found through *Resources in Education* (RIE), a monthly publication, and *Public Affairs Information Service Bulletin* (PAIS), published weekly, both accessed through a computer search. UNESCO produces numerous sources of statistics useful for research in international education. Among the most useful are *Basic Facts and Figures: International Statistics Relating to Education, Culture, and Mass Communication,* published annually; *Statistical Yearbook,* covering more than 200 countries, published annually; and *World Survey of Education,* a triennial five-volume resource on various aspects of education around the world.

The U.S. National Center for Education Statistics produces several statistical sources on education in the United States. The *Digest of Education Statistics, The Condition of Education,* and *Projections of Educational Statistics* all appear annually and are readily available in print (hard copy) as well as on ERIC microfiche. Reports of the U.S. Bureau of the Census, especially *Statistical Abstract of the United States,* available annually, include tables on public and private schools, enrollments, finances, illiteracy, dropouts, minority groups, and a variety of other topics.

Test Instruments. The identification or location of tests and measurement instruments is often a problem for researchers in the behavioral sciences and education. Buros's *Mental Measurements Yearbook,* published in eight noncumulative editions (1938-1978), is probably the most comprehensive work on commercially available tests in psychology and education. The work contains complete information on tests, reviews of tests, excerpts from test reviews, references to specific tests, bibliographies of books on testing and assessment techniques, indexes to book and test titles and names, a directory of periodicals and publishers, and a classified index of tests and reviews. The arrangement of material in the indexes and the lack of a detailed subject index make this tool somewhat difficult to use, however. You may wish to use other sources to identify a test you need before checking details and reviews of it in Buros.

Other sources can also help in identifying appropriate instruments. The following are representative of types of tools available.

A Guide to 65 Diagnostic Tests for Special Education (Compton, 1979)

Evaluations of tests useful for assessing students from kindergarten through eighth grade in the areas of language, perception and memory, general intelligence, and developmental skills.

Tests and Measurements in Child Development (Johnson, 1971 and 1976)

Covers ages from birth to eighteen years. Includes information on type of measure, variable being measured, source, description of measure, and sample items.

Assessing the Learning Disabled: Selected Instruments (Mauser, 1977)

Test categories include preschool readiness, reading readiness, survey tests, oral reading, math abilities, creativity, social adjustment, and others.

Measuring Human Behavior: Tools for the Assessment of Social Functioning (Lake, Miles, and Earle, 1973)
Systematically reviews eighty-four instruments in the general domain of normal social functioning. Also reviews other compendia of instruments.

Women and Women's Issues: A Handbook of Tests and Measures (Beere, 1979)
Describes 235 instruments covering the areas of sex roles, marital and parental roles, employee roles, multiple roles, and measures of attitudes toward women's issues.

Scales for the Measurement of Attitudes (Shaw and Wright, 1967)
Contains scales for measuring attitudes toward social practices, social issues, abstract concepts, political and religious systems, significant others, and social institutions. Exhibits of instruments are provided.

Measures for Psychological Assessment (Chun, Cobb, and French, 1975)
Indexes literature on testing in periodicals and books. Keyword index to subjects is especially useful.

Measures of Maturation: An Anthology of Early Childhood Observation Instruments (Boyer, 1973)
Includes observation systems dealing with various aspects of infancy and childhood. Systems are designed to study children individually as well as in groups. Aspects include psychomotor traits, activities, play relationships, exchanging and processing information, and interaction with environments.

Tests: A Comprehensive Reference for Assessments in Psychology, Education, and Business (Sweetland, 1984)
Over 3,000 tests are arranged by broad subjects and by subgroups within these subjects. Information given on each test includes author, title, purpose, description, type of scoring used, age range, cost, and ordering details.

Current developments and information on tests and measurement instruments can be found through *Psychological Abstracts* and in the *Education Index* under the heading "Tests and Scales." Reviews of tests can be located in the *Journal of Educational Measurement* and the *Journal of Counseling Psychology.*

Unpublished tests in the field of education and psychology are available on microfiche from the Educational Testing Service (ETS) *Tests in Microfiche.* ETS, through its Test Collection Department, is an important source of current information on measures for education. The services of ETS include the publication of bibliographies and *News on Tests,* a monthly newsletter providing current information on tests and testing, as well as a telephone reference service concerning tests.

Special Centers and Collections

Serious research is likely to require more resources and information than any one institution contains. As you proceed in your research, you will undoubtedly become aware of research centers, specialized libraries, organizations, and associations that contribute to your area of interest. Here are some references that can lead you to the specialized groups most likely to be helpful to you.

The Research Centers Directory, published biennially, lists permanent, nonprofit centers located at universities or operating independently. The centers are indexed by subject, institutional unit, and personal name. *New Research Centers* updates the bound volumes regularly.

The Encyclopedia of Associations, revised about every two years and published in three volumes, lists and describes national organizations in the United States. Organizations are grouped into seventeen major subject categories. All entries are indexed by keyword, and associations in almost every area of interest are included.

Subject Collections: A Guide to Special Book Collections and Subject Emphases as Reported by University, College, Public, and Special Libraries and Museums in the United States and Canada (Ash, 1985) provides information on collection peculiarities, size, and availability of materials to researchers by way of interlibrary loan and photoduplication.

Summary

This chapter presented information on using libraries and their personnel, services, and materials in research for a dissertation or thesis. It strongly advised you to get acquainted with your library and cultivate a research ally there who can direct, guide, and assist you in using the library's technology and resources. Learn about the services available in and through your library and how these services can help you find material in other libraries.

Explore the many kinds of reference works that your library is likely to contain. These include encyclopedias and dictionaries, handbooks and review sources, bibliographies, indexes to recent books, and other indexes and abstracting services. Sources of statistics, test instruments, and special collections may also be available. Examine in depth those sources that apply to your topic or field of interest.

Learn how to use computer searching efficiently and effectively. Find out what data bases your library can access and what information they contain. Work with a trained librarian to design a search strategy that fits your topic. With the librarian's help, you can convert a modern library's maze of technology from a forbidding obstacle to a powerful ally.

The next chapter presents advice on selecting your dissertation director and associated readers, including qualities to look for and recommended ways of working with your committee.

 FOUR

Selecting and Working
with an Advisory Committee

Selene asked Sandy Blackmur to be her dissertation director primarily because the two were such good friends. Ever since Selene had taken Dr. Blackmur's class in cultural anthropology, the two women had felt like sisters. Both had the same volatile temperament and carefree attitude toward life. Selene's topic, the bear myth of the Ainu of Japan, was not especially close to Dr. Blackmur's specialty, the American Indian, but "We'll learn together," Dr. Blackmur said. No schedules or written contracts seemed necessary between the two. Unfortunately, as time went by and Selene's dissertation was not completed, she and Dr. Blackmur both faced disapproval from several older members on Selene's committee. Selene and Dr. Blackmur also began arguing about whose fault the problem was, and Dr. Blackmur finally resigned as Selene's director.

Roberto was almost afraid to ask Dr. Gonzales to be his director. Dr. Gonzales was the department head and a world-famous theoretician in psycholinguistics. Roberto knew how busy Dr. Gonzales was; but Roberto was fascinated with a project Dr. Gonzales was conducting on language development in infants, and he hoped to use his own skill in statistics to design new test instruments to quantify the anecdotal results Dr. Gonzales was accumulating. He was surprised and delighted when Dr. Gonzales accepted him as an assistant on the project and let him do his dissertation in connection with it. The two worked out an orderly schedule of meetings, during which Roberto reported steady progress on developing his topic. Roberto rounded out his committee with Marilyn Rodell, an expert on infant behavior, and William Masterson, a statistician. Both committee members found Dr. Gonzales's reserved friendliness as appealing as Roberto did.

Selecting your advisory team is a very important step in the process of preparing your dissertation. In conjunction with this team you will refine your topic, develop your proposal, conduct your research, and write your dissertation. Ultimately, your advisory team will pass judgment on your abilities as a student, a researcher, and a professional. Therefore, you should choose your advisers with care. This chapter presents some guidelines that might be helpful in selecting and working with your advisory team.

Your Academic Adviser

Most graduate programs assign a faculty adviser to students at the beginning of their graduate program. Your academic adviser's major task is to help you formulate a program of studies that will lead to your selected career goals. Your program of studies should also be planned to cover efficiently all the requirements imposed by your department and university. Academic advisers, as distinct from dissertation directors, usually feel that they have carried out their duties if students assigned to them successfully complete preliminary or comprehensive examinations and/or meet all extra dissertation requirements.

Your Dissertation Director

Your director is likely to be the most important person on your dissertation committee—except you, of course. You usually will work more closely with your director than with anyone else, and he or she will help you coordinate your interaction with other committee members. Your director may also be able to help you deal more effectively with the department and the university.

At some institutions, unfortunately, a student has little opportunity to select a director because of departmental policy, the limited size of the adviser pool, the large number of people doing dissertations, or the specialized nature of the student's research interest. Even under the most favorable conditions, you will seldom be able to choose from among more than three or four possibilities for your director. In spite of these limitations, your choice can make a difference—so choose carefully.

If you follow the advice given earlier in this book and begin your graduate career with your sights on your dissertation, your academic adviser may well also be your dissertation director. This can be an excellent idea if your adviser has research interests that parallel your own, a personality compatible with yours, and a relationship with you that involves mutual liking and respect.

If you do not wish your adviser to be your dissertation director, begin looking for a director early in your graduate career, at more or less the same time you start looking for your dissertation topic. Become acquainted with the full range of faculty members in your program or department by taking courses they teach, attending seminars they give, and making social contacts. Students who hold research and teaching assistantships have a special avenue for working with some faculty; lacking that, you might volunteer to assist selected faculty members in order to get to know them better.

Desirable Qualities. Look for a respected member of the faculty who has standing in the professional community. Other faculty members will be more willing to work with a director they respect. To be sure, the most respected members of the faculty are also likely to be the ones who already have many advisees and outside obligations and who may therefore have little time for new advisees. A younger or less well-known faculty member may be more accessible, more interested in your topic, or more personable. Still, don't discount even the most respected and best-known member of your faculty as a possible director if his or her qualities fit your needs. Don't underestimate your own importance. He or she just might have time for you, as Dr. Gonzales did for Roberto in our opening example. Approach the professors you think are right for you and let them make the decision about whether to accept you.

Your director should be interested in your subject. Ideally, he or she should be involved in research work in the same area as yours or in a closely related one. At the least, your director should be willing to become informed about your topic and should not find it alien.

If your topic does not fit comfortably within the accepted concerns of your discipline, you may have more trouble finding a director with parallel interests. A social work student might find it difficult to find a director willing to deal with a dissertation on stress management of hypertensives, for example, unless the department has a program in medical social work. Students have occasionally changed their dissertation topics because they have been unable to find a director who could handle them.

Accessibility is another important factor to consider in selecting a director. What is the likelihood of your director being consistently available to you during the life of your project? It is very disturbing to have your director leave your institution partway through your study.

When considering someone as a possible director, check to see if that person has tenure or is likely to receive it. Ask if he or she is planning a sabbatical or other leave of absence. You should also inquire among your fellow students about this person's reputation for accessibility on a day-to-day basis. For example, is he or she receptive to telephone calls to clear up specific points of concern?

Look for a director with a reputation for reading, critiquing, and returning written material conscientiously and promptly. Here, too, the experience of other students can offer a valuable, though not infallible, guide. Different students' experiences with the same faculty member may well be somewhat different, so the wisest thing is to look for a pattern of behavior and then check that pattern against your own experience with that person.

Be realistic in forming your expectations about turnaround time for written material submitted to a director. A good rule of thumb is to allow two weeks for a response. After that, a polite inquiry may be in order.

You should also weigh rapidity of response against the thoroughness with which the faculty member reads submitted material. While you may wait longer for a chapter to be returned by a director who gives a very thorough reading, your rewriting and subsequent delays between readings may well be shortened because of the director's careful criticism.

Look for a director who will take your dissertation seriously. Seek a person with a reputation for integrity. Some students, like Selene in our opening example, gravitate to the affable person on the staff whose value system is more directed toward keeping students happy than toward producing a high-quality product. During the early stages of your dissertation an understanding, reflective faculty member might seem the best choice, but as you become more familiar with your topic, you may find that a decisive, no-nonsense type of director is more likely to get you through. Of course, a director who is both understanding and decisive is best of all.

Look for a rigorous methodologist. In education and the behavioral sciences, methodologists are sometimes accorded inordinate status and power. However, the rigor of a good methodologist can help you write a proposal and conduct a study that will not be easily challenged. If you select a director for qualities other than methodological rigor, try at least to find a committee member who has this quality.

No director is going to be perfect in every area. The best way to choose a director is to assess and rank-order your own strengths and personal needs; then rank-order the qualities you believe are most important for your director to possess. Comparing these lists can help you discover the kind of person best suited to be your director. For example, some students are so compulsively rigorous that their greatest need might be simply for unflagging support. On the other hand, a student who has brilliant ideas but tends to be sloppy about details might benefit from the discipline of a director who is something of a martinet. A student who is a first-rate statistician might best be balanced by a director who has a strong leaning toward theory. Another of Selene's mistakes was choosing a director too much like herself.

Working with Your Director. Once you have decided on the director you prefer, request a meeting with that person to discuss the reasons for your choice. Faculty members are seldom too busy to listen to students who compliment them with well-constructed personal choices.

If the faculty member you approach agrees to serve as your director, discuss how you might work best together. Try to enter into some specific agreements about the work pattern you will follow. For example, should the two of you have regular, though perhaps infrequent, meetings throughout your graduate program? Such meetings might include theoretical discussions about areas of interest that could help you focus on your ultimate research study. You probably should meet with your director at least once a semester during your course work.

Work out a sensible meeting schedule to follow during the writing of your dissertation, too. You might want to see your director about once a month as you are struggling to refine a topic and once every week or two when you begin to write your proposal.

Find out how your director prefers to work on a dissertation. Does he or she want to approve each chapter—that is, criticize or make alterations on your drafts—before allowing the remainder of your committee to read what you have written, or does your director prefer to have the whole committee read your work at once? Either method can work well; the important thing is to be sure that you and your director agree on an approach and that all your committee members are willing to operate in the same fashion.

It is a good idea to take notes on all agreements worked out with your director and to provide him or her with a written record of these agreements as well as all deadlines and other schedules agreed upon. This procedure reduces the administrative work required of your director, keeps you visible, and shows that you are well organized. Most important, by clarifying the understanding of both parties, it can help to circumvent one of the most common problems in human relations—that of unstated assumptions. It can help you keep your relationship with your director both friendly and businesslike.

Occasionally it happens that in the middle of the dissertation process, a student's director may be overwhelmed by a problem or major commitment, such as a serious illness or a new job, that makes it impossible for him or her to continue helping that student. Also, unfortunately, what may have begun as a pleasant relationship between student and director sometimes turns sour. If either of these things should happen to you, you will need to think about finding another director.

If your director has asked to be relieved for reasons that do not involve your relationship, your task is relatively straightforward. Your outgoing director will probably help you in finding a replacement. If, on the other hand, your director requests to be relieved because of feelings that your work or your interactions with him or her are unacceptable, have a serious talk with the director before you do anything. You need to understand exactly what has gone wrong before you make a decision. The same is true if you are the one who has become disenchanted.

A direct approach to the problem of personal conflict may seem embarrassing, even painful, but it is usually the best one in the long run. Try to find out how the conflict developed, then look for solutions to it. It may be due to misunderstandings that can be cleared up. Behavior changes on the part of one or both of you may minimize it. If, however, the personality clash seems insoluble, a change of directors may be the best solution for everyone concerned. Arranging such a change is not easy, but it can be done. Handle your part of the separation as maturely as you can; then don't be shy about asking another faculty member to become your new director.

Other Committee Members

Selection of the other members of your dissertation committee is sometimes subject to departmental limitations; if so, find out the policy of your department and follow it. In most cases you must find your own readers in consultation with your director.

Desirable Qualities. Select the readers on your committee carefully. A well-chosen committee continuously involved with your project will help you produce a good product. Look for readers who are interested in your topic. In general, your readers should have the same qualities as your director, but it's a good idea to assess the strengths and weaknesses of your director and seek readers who compensate for your director's deficits as well as your own. Sometimes your director will help you in your choice by outlining candidly his or her peculiar strengths and weaknesses.

If your study is data-based and your director is not a statistician, for example, you might look for a reader who has a strong statistical background. If your study is largely methodological and your director is principally a theoretician, you may wish to add a methodologist to your committee. If your study crosses several areas of inquiry and your director is expert in only one of them, look for committee members who can add expertise in the missing areas.

A graduate student named Maiko, for example, wanted to do a study dealing with the effect of social networks on the prevalence of heart disease among Type A and B personalities. Her director was an expert in social network theory but knew little about heart disease and only a modest amount about Type A and B personalities. She therefore supplemented her committee with a faculty member from the medical school of a neighboring university who was a national expert in identifying patients prone to heart disease. This outside reader proved to be exceptionally helpful as well as very interested in the results of Maiko's study.

Learn and consider each reader's preferred style of working on a dissertation. A reader who desires to be kept abreast of each development in your dissertation and wants to play a strong role in shaping your study might prove to be incompatible with a director who prefers to play a decisive role and expects readers simply to support decisions he or she has already made.

To avoid incompatibility problems, ask your director to identify faculty members with whom he or she can work comfortably.

The director generally has the final word in differences of
opinion among committee members. Sometimes, however, a
reader is more clearly an expert in a student's chosen area than
the director is. If your director will not acknowledge a colleague's proficiency, you might find yourself torn between two
different "expert" approaches to a problem.

Working with Your Committee. Try to establish good
personal relationships with each committee member. Each
member will usually have a vote as to whether your proposal or
dissertation is accepted or rejected. In addition, one of them
may become your director if your present director becomes un-
willing or unable to continue this task.

Your director may prefer to play the dominant role in
drafting your proposal or completing your dissertation. This approach tends to build a strong relationship between you and
your director, but it may do so at the expense of your involve-
ment with other committee members. If they know that this is
your director's predilection, committee members may rely too
heavily on him or her to work with you or may be hesitant to
criticize your work because doing so might seem to be criticizing your director personally.

On the other hand, if you try to keep all committee
members informed and involved by simultaneously submitting
your proposal and/or dissertation chapters to each member at
each stage of development, you risk long delays in obtaining responses from all committee members. This approach is also inefficient in that it requires several committee members to comment on the same mistakes and requires that you attempt to
integrate all comments, some of which may contradict, in your
final draft.

The best plan may be to arrange one or more meetings
with your entire committee just before your proposal defense
and another before your final defense. Such meetings offer
committee members an opportunity to establish or reestablish
a working relationship, to get to know you in the context of

your study, and to resolve diverse views. These meetings can also help you become aware of any sharp disagreements that cannot be resolved, allowing you time to make major study revisions or replace a member who is not in agreement with the rest of the committee.

No matter what policies are in effect at your school regarding approvals for your proposal or dissertation, you should obtain signatures of approval from all the members of your committee. Such a goal may require you to revise your topic, try to reconcile apparently irreconcilable perspectives, adjust your methodology, change your analyses, alter your population, or reformulate your theory. In the end, however, it is worth the effort to receive the unanimous approval of your committee members. In addition, obtaining these approvals in writing can protect you by providing evidence that your topic and plan were initially accepted by the entire committee in case changes occur in your committee at a later date.

You should expect to have to revise both your proposal and your dissertation repeatedly—probably at least six times. You will probably understand and agree with the reasoning behind most suggested modifications. There may be times, however, when you disagree strongly with one or more of your committee members about a proposed change. Try first to work out differences with each member individually. If you find that you cannot, use your director as a mediator. Request a meeting with your committee if the problem is a critical one. Present reasons for your point of view in a logical and dignified manner. Do not be obstinate, but remember that you don't need to agree to every change suggested by a committee member. If you believe you have good reason to maintain your position, hold your ground.

Sometimes a particular committee member proves to be incompatible with the others or refuses to share in a general approval of your work. If this happens, you are faced with the choice of making further accommodations for that member or replacing him or her on your committee. If a substitute is available, the easiest thing is usually to politely but firmly excuse the difficult member. You are better off with a new member than a hostile one.

Ask your director's advice, then follow through with both direct contact and correspondence with the member you wish to replace. The matter must be handled delicately, but it is not impossible; it is certainly easier than replacing your director, for example. You are quite likely to find that the conflicting member is glad to be relieved of his or her difficult role.

As you struggle with the difficulties and inconveniences of doing a dissertation, you will be offered plenty of opportunities to be annoyed with everybody, including your committee members. This one may not be punctual; that one may not read what you have written fast enough to suit you. Any of them can make a mistake. You will need to show patience and forgiveness in dealing with your committee, just as you may sometimes need to hope for their patience and forgiveness in dealing with you.

Summary

Your dissertation director and committee can make a great difference in both the success of your dissertation and your ease in producing it. You should therefore select these people carefully.

It is especially important to choose the right director. Begin looking for a director early in your graduate career. If you are not planning to use your academic adviser as your director, get to know a wide range of other faculty members. Try to find a director who is a respected member of the faculty and who also has a reputation for being accessible to students. Seek someone who is interested in your subject, gets along well with you, and is conscientious about being both thorough and relatively prompt in critiques. If possible, the strengths and weaknesses of your director should balance your own.

In working with your director, plan a mutually agreeable meeting schedule and way of working on the dissertation. Putting agreements and schedules into written form can keep your relationship businesslike and help to avoid misunderstandings.

Your committee should have the same general characteristics as your director but should also include members who can make up for any lack of expertise in your director and yourself. Ask for your director's advice in selecting committee members in order to obtain a good balance of skills and avoid incompatibility.

Try to maintain a good relationship with all your committee members and work out a plan that will keep everyone informed of your progress in an efficient manner. It is a good idea to meet with your committee just before your proposal defense and again before your final dissertation defense.

It is important to gain your committee's unanimous approval for your proposal and dissertation. However, you do not need to accept every change a committee member suggests. Hold your ground if you feel you have good reason to object to a change. If committee members make mistakes, treat them with patience and forgiveness.

Chapter Five provides detailed instructions for preparing the first two chapters of your proposal. In it you will learn how to state the purpose of your study, establish a context for the study, and review the research literature related to your topic.

 FIVE

Writing the Proposal: Introduction and Literature Chapters

Michael's dissertation topic was the comparison of the effectiveness of two psychotropic drugs in controlling schizophrenic symptoms in a hospital and an outpatient setting. He began the introductory chapter of his proposal by placing this topic in the context of research on external factors that influenced the drug dosage necessary to effectively control schizophrenic symptoms. After stating the purpose of his study, he named several hypotheses that he planned to test, including the hypothesis that a smaller dose of a psychotropic drug would be needed to produce a given degree of control of schizophrenic symptoms in an outpatient setting than would be needed to provide the same degree of control in a hospital setting. His introductory chapter also explained what he meant by such terms as "control" and "schizophrenic symptoms"; listed some assumptions and limitations of his study; and described the study's significance for more accurate prescription of drug dosage for schizophrenic patients.

Michael's review of literature chapter described in more detail the context he had summarized in his introduction to the problem. It also included the theoretical framework for his study. It discussed previous research on the effectiveness of different doses of the two drugs he planned to study and also on the effect of external factors, particularly setting, on schizophrenics' reaction to psychotropic drugs. It listed several ways of measuring certain schizophrenic symptoms and described their use in other drug-related studies. Michael arranged his chapter to highlight studies that supported his hypotheses, but he also pointed out weaknesses in those studies and explained how his own project might compensate for these weaknesses.

After you have defined the problem you intend to investigate for your dissertation, you need to develop a research plan that specifies exactly how you will proceed with the study. Normally, you will describe the nature of your study and your research plan in a formal document called a proposal. Approval of the proposal following a successful defense of it before your committee usually constitutes official permission from the university to begin your research.

This chapter and the following one present guidelines for the preparation of a proposal. The sections described in them will appear in most proposals. Some of the specific guidelines, however, pertain mostly to quantitative research studies. You may want to consult additional books on dissertation preparation, such as those of Madsen (1983) and Allen (1973), if your study is qualitative or historical. A brief discussion of these different types of research is given in Appendix B.

Organizing Your Proposal

The proposal forms the basis on which your dissertation committee and, ultimately, your university will evaluate your planned research. You should develop your proposal in close consultation with your committee. Such consultation can spare you unpleasant surprises at the time of your proposal defense.

Before developing a full proposal, prepare a one- or two-page synopsis of your topic and tentative research plan. This synopsis will enable your dissertation director and committee to give preliminary reactions to your ideas. These reactions, in turn, should provide helpful guidance for developing the complete proposal.

Format of the Proposal. The exact form for the proposal is usually specified by your department. Your director should have information regarding the required or preferred format. Length expectations can vary from a few pages to something approximating the first three chapters of the eventual dissertation. Reviewing approved proposals written by other students in your department can also teach you about format.

The type of study may also determine the format and length of your proposal. It certainly will affect the proposal's content. A proposal for a study employing strictly qualitative methods is likely to be very different from one for a study employing quantitative methods. Qualitative methods emphasize induction, description, and the study of environments and perceptions. A proposal for a study based primarily on such methods would most likely be a rather brief general statement of approach with no extensive literature base and no hypotheses. The research design may constantly evolve as data are collected (Bogdan and Biklen, 1982).

The format presented in this chapter, however, is intended to produce a detailed proposal having a specific focus supported by an extensive literature base and one or more hypotheses. The proposal also includes a specific research design with descriptions of sampling procedures, instrumentation, research procedures, and data analysis. Such proposals are common in the behavioral sciences.

Most proposals contain an introductory chapter, a review of literature chapter, a method chapter, references, and, if needed, one or more appendices. Each chapter is likely to be divided into sections, as shown in Exhibit 2. The section on references usually includes complete bibliographic information only for those sources actually cited in the proposal, although in some cases a more extensive bibliography is appropriate. The appendix normally contains copies of instruments, detailed instructions, instructional material, form letters, and similar documents.

Long or Short? Given the option of producing a very

Exhibit 2. Outline of a Proposal.

Introduction
- Introduction to the Problem
- Purpose of the Study
- Hypotheses and Research Questions
- Definition of Terms (if applicable)
- Significance of the Study
- Assumptions and Limitations

Review of the Literature
(If brief, this section could be incorporated into the first section of the proposal.)

Method
- Population and Sample
- Instruments
- Materials (if applicable)
- Tasks (if applicable)
- Treatment (if applicable)
- Pilot Study (if applicable)
- Procedures
- Design and Data Analysis

References
Appendix (if applicable)

---

brief proposal or a very detailed one, many students might elect, on first thought, to do the brief one because their research plans are still relatively undeveloped; however, a more detailed proposal has several advantages. First, preparing a detailed proposal requires you to explore and describe fully the problem you intend to investigate, its theoretical framework, and its associated literature base. A well-developed theoretical framework and review of literature enable better committee evaluation of the worth of your study than do brief synopses. Even if you are expected to produce only a brief proposal, you will need to conduct a review of literature broad enough to allow you to define the problem adequately and explain its theoretical framework. Thus, the additional work involved in producing a detailed proposal is mainly in structuring and writing, not in research. Since you will need to write chapters on theoretical framework and review of literature for your dissertation anyway, the time you spend doing this for your proposal will not be wasted.

Another advantage is that in a more developed proposal you will be required to make explicit your decisions regarding methodology, particularly data analysis, whereas in a brief proposal, methodology might receive superficial treatment. For example, in a brief proposal you might state simply that you will use a certain statistical analysis, such as the analysis of variance or regression analysis, without considering all the ramifications of that particular analytical method. In a more developed proposal, however, you will be expected to provide a description of your use of the proposed analysis that is sufficiently detailed to allow proper evaluation of your entire data analysis strategy. This detailed description of methodology can provide an excellent blueprint to guide you through your study.

Third, by developing a detailed proposal you will have virtually completed the first three chapters of your dissertation. Only a few changes, usually minor, will need to be made for the final draft: the addition of any recent or previously overlooked references; changes in tense, usually from the future to the past or the present; and perhaps the rewriting of sections of the method chapter to reflect changes that occurred after the completed proposal. Thus, by doing a substantial amount of writing prior to actually beginning your study, you will free more time to devote later to data analysis, data interpretation, and the writing of the rest of the dissertation.

The following discussion assumes that you are writing a detailed proposal. Thus, the major parts of the proposal are referred to as chapters, each containing several sections. A shorter proposal might simply have only sections and subsections.

Introductory Chapter

The introductory chapter of your proposal provides an orientation to your study. In it you describe the problem you plan to investigate, state the purpose of your study, indicate the questions and hypotheses you will address, and tell why the study is important. A synopsis of the theoretical framework underlying your study forms a major part of the introductory chapter.

Introduction to the Problem. The first section of your introductory chapter contains a description and analysis of the problem you plan to investigate in your study. It is really a formal version of the process you went through in choosing and developing your topic.

You might begin this section by identifying the context within which you will conduct your study and giving any background information needed to clarify the context. Next, provide a clear and succinct description, citing relevant sources, of how present knowledge about the problem has evolved and what issues remain unsolved. For example, suppose your study involves the comparison of various methods for establishing standards or minimum passing scores for competency tests used by the Coast Guard. You would need to explain: (1) the nature of the tests used by the Coast Guard, (2) how the Coast Guard currently determines minimum passing scores, and (3) why there is a need to examine other methods for determining minimum passing scores.

Aim your description toward the particular focus you have decided to take in your study. Include discussion of independent, dependent, control, and moderator variables that are important to consider in the study.

All issues discussed in this section and all sources cited should also be included in the review of literature chapter. In fact, it is often easier to write the review of literature chapter first, then abstract its most salient points and order them in a way that describes the problem and provides its rationale.

Purpose of the Study. A section on the purpose of the study follows the description and analysis of the problem. This section should indicate precisely which aspects of the problem you intend to examine. You should identify the variables that will be considered and state the major questions your study is intended to answer. Problems for investigation may be expressed either as questions or as statements. Each problem may be divided into several subproblems.

Let's use Koelle's dissertation as an example again. As you may recall, he intended to investigate the relative importance of self-concept and locus of control in predicting the achievement of deaf adolescents. His review of literaure indicated that deaf adolescents, as a group, performed differently on measures of locus of control than did adolescents with normal hearing. He also learned that deaf adolescents have some difficulty in understanding sentences containing certain syntactic structures. Some possible subproblems for his research might be:

Subproblem 1: The first subproblem is to determine the relative importance of self-concept and locus of control in predicting the achievement of deaf adolescents. (statement)

Subproblem 2: Is the relative importance of self-concept and locus of control in predicting achievement the same for hearing adolescents as for deaf adolescents? (question)

Subproblem 3: What effect does the removal of syntax troublesome to deaf adolescents from self-concept and locus-of-control items in questionnaires have on the relative importance of these variables in predicting the achievement of such adolescents? (question)

The subproblems stated here illustrate different forms this kind of statement can take. In your study, you should express all subproblems the same way, as questions or as statements, for uniformity. Your statement of the problem should be complete, listing all the important variables and circumstances you will consider in your study. For example, other variables that influence the achievement of deaf adolescents are whether the child's parents are hearing or deaf, the school the child attends, and the child's sex. None of these variables was of primary interest to the researcher, so they were not included explicitly in the subproblem statements. However, because of their importance, they needed to be identified at some point in this section. That might be done, after stating the subproblems, in a paragraph something like this:

Regression analysis will be employed to examine each of the subproblems. The dependent variable in each regression equation will be the standardized achievement score. In addition to self-concept and locus of control, other predictors will include parent hearing status, school attended, and sex. These latter predictors are included strictly for control and will be entered into the regression equations prior to self-concept and locus of control.

Hypotheses and Research Questions. Hypotheses are conjectures, subject to verification, that offer possible solutions to questions associated with the problem under investigation. Research questions ask about relationships among variables; hypotheses speculate about the nature of these relationships. The following are examples of hypotheses:

Hypothesis 1:   Parental power is perceived to be more uniformly distributed among mother and father by adolescents with working mothers than by adolescents with nonworking mothers.

Hypothesis 2:   The interpersonal communication competence of adults is directly related to their interpersonal support systems.

Hypothesis 3:   When asked to recall experiences shared with close friends, younger children will recall a higher percentage of action-based content than will older children.

Hypotheses are informed conjectures based on theory or previous research, not merely wild guesses. Most studies have hypotheses, but some do not. Some problems are exploratory and are based on little, if any, theory or previous research. For research questions associated with these problems, it is not always possible to formulate hypotheses, since theoretical support cannot be provided for them. You should state hypotheses only for those research questions for which you are able to provide a rationale from your theoretical framework.

Usually a study has one or two general hypotheses from which specific hypotheses or predictions can be derived. Confirmation of each specific hypothesis provides evidence for the confirmation of the general hypothesis. For example, a general hypothesis might be, "Teaching science to elementary school children is more effective when discovery methods, rather than traditional didactic methods, are used." Derived hypotheses could focus on differences between discovery and didactic groups on standardized tests, attitudes toward science, knowledge of process as opposed to simply facts, and transfer of knowledge to events in daily life. They should help make explicit the way the researcher plans to define and measure "effectiveness."

In this section of the proposal, you should write all hypotheses as research hypotheses rather than as statistical hypotheses. A research hypothesis predicts the nature of the relationship being examined in rather general, nonquantitative terms; a statistical hypothesis is a translation of the research hypothesis in terms of the statistical parameters of the population being studied. The following are examples of research hypotheses and their corresponding statistical hypotheses:

Research	*Statistical*
Children taught by the discovery method will be more favorable toward science than children taught by the didactic method.	The mean score on a science appreciation rating scale of children taught by the discovery method is greater than the mean score of children taught by the didactic method.
The working status of mothers has a greater influence on boys' perceptions of mother as a role model than on girls' perceptions of mother as a role model.	The difference between the mean scores on the Parent Identification Scale for boys of working mothers and those of nonworking mothers is greater than the difference between the mean scores for girls of working mothers and those of nonworking mothers.

Statistical hypotheses are written either as null hypotheses or alternative hypotheses. A null hypothesis specifies no difference or no relationship between variables. If a null hypothesis can be rejected on the basis of the data, then its alternative hypothesis is assumed to be supported. Since the alternative hypothesis normally corresponds to the research hypothesis but is stated in statistical terms, the same decision that is made about the alternative hypothesis is made about the research hypothesis. The statistical hypotheses given above are stated as alternative hypotheses. The null hypotheses corresponding to each of them are:

Null Hypothesis: The mean score on a science appreciation rating scale of children taught by the discovery method is equal to the mean score of children taught by the didactic method.

Null Hypothesis: The difference between the mean scores on the Parent Identification Scale for boys of working mothers and those of nonworking mothers is equal to the difference between the mean scores for girls of working mothers and girls of nonworking mothers.

These null hypotheses would be tested statistically using the data from the respective studies. If either is rejected, and if the mean scores observed in each sample agree with the prediction made in the respective alternative hypothesis, then the alternative hypothesis would be assumed to be supported. The researcher would then most likely assume that the corresponding research hypothesis is confirmed. For example, suppose the first null hypothesis given above is rejected. If the observed mean score of the discovery group is greater than the observed mean score of the didactic group, then the alternative hypothesis would be supported. The researcher would then claim that the research hypothesis, since it corresponds to the alternative hypothesis, is confirmed. However, the null hypothesis would also be rejected if the mean score on a science appreciation rating scale of children taught by the discovery method was less than the mean score of children taught by the didactic method. This was not anticipated by the researcher, so in this case neither the alternative nor the research hypothesis would be confirmed. Should this situation occur, critics of the research would seriously question the theoretical basis of the study or the judgments made by the researcher in designing the study.

Definition of Terms. Definitions of all important terms should be provided in this section. You should define operationally any term that lacks precise meaning, such as self-concept, creativity, locus of control, biased test item, discovery method, open classroom, attitude toward school, affectionate behavior, and preference for an activity. An operational definition states explicitly the manner in which a term is being measured or manipulated. Here are some examples of operational definitions:

Locus of control—the sense of personal control over the events in an individual's life, as measured by the score on the Rotter Internal-External Locus of Control Scale.

Affectionate behavior—the tendency of a teacher to smile at, or exchange pleasantries with, a student as measured by the number of times these actions occur during a normal class period.

High Discovery condition—a self-directed learning situation where no teacher guidance is provided, such as a situation in which students at a computer terminal are given operating instructions and a few basic commands but must learn other commands and eventually write a simple program on their own.

In addition to reducing ambiguity and increasing objectivity, operational definitions reflect the way you have interpreted your hypotheses and research questions and the way you have chosen to address them. For example, defining attitude toward school as a score on a self-report inventory rather than as actual participation in school activities will affect the interpretation of any hypothesis you make concerning attitude toward school.

Significance of the Study. This section should describe

the importance of your study and the contribution to knowledge that you expect the study to make. Present evidence for the theoretical significance of the study and also for its practical significance, if any. Theoretical contributions include contributions you expect to make to the establishment or verification of theories or models, or to an existing body of research. Arguments for theoretical contributions should be developed from the literature. Arguments for practical significance may focus on the impact of your results on the profession or on the solution of practical problems.

Assumptions and Limitations. In this section you should list the major assumptions underlying your study, particularly those on which your hypotheses are based. Provide a rationale to support any assumption that is likely to be challenged. (The assumptions included in this section are not those on which your statistical analyses will be based. Those assumptions should be discussed in the section of the proposal dealing with analysis of data.) For example, assumptions that might appear in this section of the proposal for the science-teaching study include the following:

- behavior is characterized by some degree of consistency;
- the behavior of interest is observable and properly measured;
- all individuals in a group benefit equally from a group treatment;
- subjects have the ability to report their perceptions accurately;
- the time allotted for the treatment is adequate to produce the desired effects;
- all important variables influencing the dependent variable have been controlled or explicitly included in the design;
- student achievement is a function of both in-school and out-of-school factors.

This section should also describe any limitations of the study that may have a serious effect on the interpretation of the findings or on the generalizability of the results. Limitations occur because of design constraints or failure to meet assumptions. Design constraints usually involve some aspect of sampling, measurement, control, or model misspecification. Examples of limitations are samples consisting only of volunteers, measurement instruments with inadequate or unknown validity, and failure to include important variables in the design. Often limitations do not become apparent until the study is completed, but any important limitations imposed on the study in the planning stage should be mentioned in the proposal. All important limitations should be included in this section of the final dissertation as well. Sometimes a separate section on limitations is warranted if the list of limitations is accompanied by an extensive commentary.

Review of Literature Chapter

The review of literature chapter is the heart of your proposal. It contains the formal description of the theoretical framework of your study. In this chapter you establish the foundation for the study by providing complete documentation for the study's context, problem, hypotheses, significance, and (in many cases) methodology.

The review of literature should be a well-integrated discussion of the theory and previous research relevant to the problem under investigation. In this chapter you tell the reader what is known regarding the problem and what still needs to be researched. You describe relevant studies: who completed them and when, what approaches were used, and what was found. A good review of literature is more than an annotated bibliography, however; it is a critical synthesis. In it you demonstrate how previous studies are related to each other and to your study by identifying similarities and differences in the studies, discriminating between relevant and irrelevant information, and indicating weaknesses in previous work.

Organizing the Chapter. In conducting your search of the literature, you should have determined the following things:

• the relevance of existing theories to your problem;

- previous empirical studies that are relevant to your problem;
- other studies and issues that must be reviewed to provide a broad context for your study;
- verified facts related to your problem, based on hypotheses that previous studies have confirmed or on assumptions made by previous studies that seem to be reasonable;
- specific research needs that you or others have identified;
- all important variables that need to be considered;
- functional relationships that exist among the variables;
- specific methodologies that others have employed;
- instruments that others have employed and their apparent appropriateness; and
- the populations studied by others and specific results for each population.

In addition, for each study that you have reviewed, you should have examined carefully the study's rationale, the manner in which the study was conducted, and the appropriateness of the data analysis and the researcher's interpretations and conclusions. Now you must organize all this information and present it in an orderly fashion.

The organization of your review of literature will reflect your understanding of the theoretical framework of your study. The review should deal first with the general context of your problem and relevant theories, then proceed logically to the specific issues immediately relevant to your study. This narrowing of focus is much like the delimiting you probably went through in selecting your topic.

Every problem fits into a larger context. This context, as described in your proposal, should provide a framework that can help readers understand your problem and interpret your results. For example, a study of the effect of different parole officer personalities (warm and affectionate versus cold and domineering) on the attitudes of black parolees toward the criminal justice system could fit into several larger contexts, including the effect of different parole officer personalities on all parolees' attitudes toward the criminal justice system and the factors that influence the attitudes of black parolees toward the criminal justice system.

Make an outline showing the dimensions of your problem that you wish to describe. The points of your outline can become the subheadings for the first draft of your review chapter. Next, sort the studies you have reviewed into the appropriate categories and list the issues under each category that you intend to discuss.

The discussion under each subheading normally will begin with an overview, including any necessary definitions. General theories that apply can be explained next, followed by a review of pertinent research studies. For example, a possible organization of subheadings and their discussion for the study of the relationship between self-concept, locus of control, and the achievement of deaf adolescents might look like this:

Self-Concept

- Overview and Definitions
- Theories of Self-Concept
- Relationship to Achievement
- Studies with Deaf Populations

Locus of Control

- Overview and Definitions
- Theories of Personal Control
- Relationship to Achievement
- Relationship to Self-Concept
- Studies with Deaf Populations

Research with Deaf Subjects

- Structural and Vocabulary Problems
- Correlates of Achievement
- Parent Hearing Status

Psychometric Issues

- Rewriting Items: Effect on Reliability and Validity
- Testing of Deaf Populations

Writing the Chapter. After you are satisfied with your outline, you are ready to write the review chapter. For models of appropriate writing style and organization, study the well-integrated reviews of literature regularly found in *Annual Review of Anthropology,* the *Review of Educational Research, The Yearbook of Psychiatry and Applied Mental Health,* the *Annual Review of Psychology,* and the *Annual Review of Sociology.* You should also examine the dissertations produced by students from your department, especially those directed by your major adviser, for sample reviews of literature.

Be selective in writing your review. Some dimensions of your problem may have hundreds of studies associated with them, and it would be redundant and wasteful to describe all or even a modest percentage of them. Criteria for including a study should be its relative importance, when it was completed (include a balance of older and more recent studies), and the appropriateness of its information for your study. Selectivity applies to the length of individual study descriptions, too; the more important a study is to your topic, the more detailed a description it deserves.

Your review chapter should end with a brief summary of the literature—an overview of all the salient points of the review that makes the rationale for your study and its hypotheses apparent. Draw on this summary when preparing the discussion of the problem in your introductory chapter and describing the rationale for each of your hypotheses.

This chapter of your proposal is likely to be the most difficult to write. It may need to go through several drafts. If possible, have someone—preferably an expert in your field—review the chapter after you have completed what you consider your final draft. At the very least, put the chapter away for a week and then reexamine it with a critical eye.

Summary

The proposal is the formal document in which you describe in detail the nature of your study and your research plan. It is the basis on which your dissertation committee and, ultimately, your university will evaluate your planned research. Because the proposal is a blueprint showing exactly how you will conduct your study, it can also provide invaluable guidance to you when you actually begin your research work. For all these reasons, it is very important to prepare your proposal carefully.

Prefer a detailed proposal to a brief one. A detailed proposal requires you to thoroughly understand your proposed study and its theoretical framework. It also provides better guidance to both you and your committee. The three chapters of a detailed proposal usually can be transformed into the first three chapters of your dissertation with very little additional work. Thus, once you have prepared a detailed proposal, you have completed a large part of the work on your dissertation.

Check with your dissertation director to find out what proposal format you will be expected to use. The exact format will depend partly on the nature of your study. A detailed proposal usually contains three chapters: introduction, review of the literature, and method. In addition, it contains references and may contain an appendix. This chapter provided specific guidance for preparing the first two chapters of the proposal; the method chapter is covered in Chapter Six.

The introductory chapter of your proposal provides an orientation to your study. In it you describe the problem you plan to study, state the purpose of your study, list the hypotheses and research questions you will address, define any important terms, tell why your study is significant, and list the assumptions and limitations involved in it.

The review of literature chapter is the heart of your proposal. It contains a formal description of the theoretical framework of your study. It should be a well-integrated analysis and synthesis of your reading, not merely an annotated bibliography. This chapter should provide complete documentation for your study's context, problem, hypotheses, significance, and (in many cases) methodology.

The next chapter provides guidance for preparing the method chapter of your proposal.

 SIX

Writing the Proposal: Method Chapter

Meiling planned to do her dissertation on the effect of employment and of parental attitudes about employment on self-reported marriage satisfaction in women. In the method chapter of her proposal, Meiling explained that she would choose her sample from a population of volunteers who answered an advertisement she planned to place in several women's magazines. She would use stratified random sampling to help control for such variables as socioeconomic class. She discussed the limits to representativeness in her sample that were caused by her having to use volunteers.

Meiling felt that none of the currently available test instruments devoted to measuring marriage satisfaction quite suited her needs, for reasons she had previously explained in her review of literature chapter. She planned, therefore, to design her own questionnaire. She described the proposed questionnaire in the instruments section of her method chapter. Later in the chapter she also described a pilot study she planned to conduct to test the validity and reliability of her questionnaire as compared to existing ones. She explained how she would administer her questionnaire and the statistical techniques she planned to use in analyzing its results.

Your research design is the plan and structure of your study, a blueprint of the procedures by which you will address your research questions and interpret your results. Much of the terminology associated with research designs originated from experimental research, but your study will need to have a design even if it is not strictly experimental.

The third chapter of your proposal should contain a detailed description of your research design. In this chapter you will describe the following:

- your population and sample, including the sampling procedures used;
- your planned instrumentation;
- your research procedures; and
- the methods you intend to use in collection and analysis of data.

A more detailed description of each of these aspects follows.

Population and Sample

The first section of your method chapter should describe carefully the population from which you intend to select the participants for your study. It should also describe your sampling plan in detail, specifying the type of sampling procedure, the actual conduct of the sampling, and the number of individuals needed. If your research design permits random assignment to groups, indicate how that will be accomplished. Indicate whether the individuals will be volunteers or required to participate, and from whom (if anyone) permission for participation will be required as well as how it will be obtained.

Population. A population is a group of individuals who share one or more attributes. The more attributes the individuals share, the more restricted the population is. The population of elementary school children in the United States is more restricted than the population of all human beings, and the population of sixth-grade students in urban public schools in the United States is more restricted still. Theoretically, the population you choose places constraints on the sample; however, often an appropriate sample is identified first and the population defined on the basis of the sample. For example, a school may permit you to use only students from fourth grade in your study. You would then define your population in terms of the available sample—namely, fourth-grade students.

Choice of population will affect the generalizability of your results. You can generalize your findings to the most restricted population from which you sampled, assuming your sample is representative of that population. You may be able to generalize further to a less restricted population if you can provide a satisfactory rationale. Generally, you should choose the least restricted population appropriate for your problem that will enable you to obtain a representative sample without great hardship.

Sample. Two desirable characteristics of a sample are representativeness and independence of units. Representativeness enables results from the sample to be generalized to the population. Independence of units, whether individuals or groups, is required by most of the statistical procedures you are likely to use to analyze your data. The major sampling procedures that provide both representativeness and independence are random sampling, stratified random sampling, cluster sampling, and, in some cases, systematic sampling.

Random sampling is the process of selecting individuals (or groups) from a population so that each person (or group) has an equal chance of being selected. *Stratified random sampling* is random sampling from subpopulations (strata) within the population of interest. The subpopulations are determined by variables, ordinarily identified in the review of literature, needed to control sources of variation influencing the dependent variable. These variables are attributes that are not shared by all individuals in the population in the same way. For example, for the population of sixth-grade students in urban public schools, such variables include socioeconomic status, race, and sex. Stratified random sampling usually provides a more representative sample than strictly random sampling does and thus is usually the sampling procedure of choice. Both random sampling and stratified random sampling are easily accomplished by using a table of random numbers (see Shavelson, 1981, pp. 10-12).

Cluster sampling ordinarily is a multistage procedure in which successively smaller units are sampled until the desired unit is obtained. For example, if individual students are the desired unit, then school districts might be sampled first, followed by a sampling of schools within districts, classrooms within schools, and finally students within classrooms. Cluster sampling is particularly efficient when the target population is large.

In *systematic sampling,* every nth individual from some predetermined list of the population is selected. If the predetermined list contains any concealed periodic bias, this type of sample may not be representative of the population. For example, bias will occur if every fifth name tends to be from a middle to upper socioeconomic group and socioeconomic status is related to the variables in the study.

Representativeness of a sample is jeopardized by individuals who refuse to participate in the study and by volunteers. Nonresponse can be a serious problem in studies using surveys or mailed questionnaires; the severity of the problem is determined to some extent by the amount of nonresponse. You can minimize nonresponse problems by providing replacements from another sample created when the primary sample was selected and, especially in the case of mailings, by following the initial questionnaires with reminders after a few weeks. Volunteers will also affect the representativeness of the sample if volunteers and nonvolunteers differ with respect to the variables in the study. The use of volunteers will usually limit the generalizability of your findings. Try to avoid using volunteers and to ensure full participation of the individuals sampled whenever possible.

The independence of the sampling units is jeopardized whenever you sample larger units than those you intend to use in your analysis. If individuals are to be used in the analysis, your sampling units should be individuals, not groups. If groups constitute the sampling units, then the unit of analysis for your statistical procedures should also be groups.

Choosing Your Sample. The number of individuals selected for a sample should be large enough to minimize sampling error and to provide adequate power for whatever statistical procedure you intend to use for data analysis. *Sampling error* occurs when a sample statistic is different from the population parameter that it estimates. The degree of sampling error depends on the variability of scores in the population and the number of observations in the sample. For samples of equal size, sampling error decreases as the homogeneity of the population increases. Thus larger samples are required to keep sampling error to a minimum in very heterogeneous populations, while smaller samples are sufficient for homogeneous populations. The standard error of the parameter estimator provides a measure of the sampling error.

The *power* of a statistical procedure is the likelihood that the procedure will properly detect a significant effect. Power is formally defined as the probability of rejecting the null hypothesis given that it is false. Power depends upon the level of significance, the size of the effect, and the size of the sample.

The *level of significance* is defined as the probability of committing a Type I error, which is falsely rejecting a null hypothesis that is true. The level of significance is represented by the lower-case Greek letter α and ordinarily has a value of .05 or .01. The *size of the effect*, usually expressed as a ratio, represents the difference that actually exists between parameters of interest relative to some index of variability. For example, if you were examining the difference between the means of two groups, the effect size would be the absolute value of the difference between the population means of the two groups divided by the population standard deviation. Since the effect size is expressed strictly in terms of population parameters, it must always be estimated. One way to estimate the effect size is to consult previous research or conduct a pilot study. Another approach is to decide on the minimum effect size that you would want to detect if the difference between the parameters was at least that large. An excellent treatment of power is provided by Cohen (1969).

You can use the relationship between power, level of significance, effect size, and sample size to help you determine an adequate sample size for your study. If two of these quantities are held constant, the other two will vary in a predictable way. For example, if the level of significance and the effect size are fixed, power varies directly with the sample size; that is, larger samples have higher power. Thus, a recommended strategy for determining a minimum sample size is as follows:

1. Choose a value for power; .80 is reasonable in most cases. Larger values of power ordinarily require a very large sample. Smaller values, especially those less than .50, are less desirable.
2. Choose the level of significance, say .05 or .01 (or any other probability value that you consider reasonable).
3. Estimate the effect size from the literature or from a pilot study, or choose the smallest effect size of practical significance to you.
4. Calculate the sample size determined by your choices in the first three steps. Cohen provides extensive tables to assist with the calculations in this step.
5. If the resulting sample size is too large for your resources, either reduce the desired level of power somewhat or increase the effect size (larger effects are easier to detect than smaller ones) until you reach an acceptable compromise.

Using this strategy and balancing the resulting sample size and power against feasibility considerations will enable you to provide a rationale for the sample size you choose rather than seeming to pull the number out of a hat.

A complete treatment of sampling procedures is found in most introductory behavioral science statistics textbooks, such as Glass and Stanley (1970) and Shavelson (1981), or in textbooks devoted to sampling procedures, such as Cochran (1977) and Williams (1978). Raj (1972) provides a good treatment of sampling procedures for surveys.

Instruments

This section of your method chapter should describe the measurement instruments or procedures you plan to use to provide the data for your study. Each description should include the name, author, type (for example, questionnaire, Likert scale,

achievement test, criterion-referenced test, observation schedule, semantic differential, structured interview), purpose, number of items, and scoring of the instrument or procedure. In
addition, you will need to provide evidence for its validity and
reliability, being sure to identify the type of validity (content,
criterion-referenced, construct) and reliability (internal consistency, equivalence, stability) and the source for the evidence.
If an instrument contains subscales or subtests, these also
should be identified, including the number of items in each subscale and the reliability estimate for each subscale. If possible,
include a copy of each instrument in the appendix to your proposal.

The measurement instrument or procedure that you
choose must be both *valid* (measure what it purports to measure) and *reliable* (produce consistent scores). Validity is more
important than reliability, since scores that are consistent but
do not measure the variable of interest are useless. On the other
hand, reliability is necessary for validity; an instrument or procedure that does not produce reliable measures cannot produce
valid ones. Other important considerations are the appropriateness of an instrument for the age group of interest, its ease of
administration, and the amount of time needed to complete it.

Validity. The validity of a measurement is not an immu-
table characteristic; it depends on how the instrument is used.
The type of information sought, the population to which it is
administered, and the criterion measure used affect the interpretation of an instrument's validity. If all are appropriate for your
study, you should provide evidence for the three major types of
validity: content, criterion-referenced or predictive, and construct.

Content validity indicates how well the material included
in the instrument represents all possible material that could
have been included. Content validity is particularly important
for achievement and proficiency measures and for some observational measures like social interaction scales. *Criterion-referenced validity* indicates how well the instrument correlates with
some criterion external to it. Criterion-referenced validity is important in prediction studies, in identifying important control

variables for a study, and in identifying predictors for a regression analysis or covariates for an analysis of covariance. *Construct validity* indicates how well the instrument measures the theoretical concept, called a construct or trait, that is assumed to explain the behavior represented in the instrument. Construct validity is important when you make inferences about performance on a general concept from the performance on a set of items.

The following example illustrates how different types of validity estimates might be involved in the same study. Suppose you plan to measure self-esteem and use this to predict achievement. You would adopt a definition of self-esteem and generate a set of characteristics or behaviors that you would assume were representative of positive and negative self-esteem. You would then locate or construct an instrument that contained questions involving these characteristics and behaviors. The content validity of the instrument would be the extent to which the questions representatively sampled the possible characteristics and behaviors. Construct validity would be how well the instrument actually measured self-esteem. Criterion-referenced validity would be how well the self-esteem instrument predicted achievement.

Estimating the content validity and criterion-referenced validity of an instrument is straightforward; estimating the construct validity is difficult. Content validity is normally established by a judgmental process using experts. Often descriptive statistics like the percent agreement of the judges' ratings are used as indices of content validity; however, content validity often is simply described without quantification. Criterion-referenced validity is represented by the correlation coefficient between the instrument and the criterion of interest; it is a function of the particular criterion used. Criterion-referenced validity coefficients rarely exceed .60 and commonly are in the .30 to .50 range.

Construct validity is usually estimated by a combination of logical and empirical procedures. The logical procedures involve examining other possible explanations for the performance on the instrument, attempting to eliminate systematically each explanation so that only the presumed one remains. This method is sometimes referred to as rival hypotheses (Cronbach, 1971). The empirical procedures usually are based on correlations and involve factor analysis, simple correlational analysis comparing other instruments that supposedly measure the same construct, and convergent and discriminant validity estimates using the multitrait, multimethod procedure of Campbell and Fiske (1959). No single procedure provides sufficient evidence for construct validity, and evidence is ordinarily accumulated through repeated uses of the instrument over a period of time. Cronbach (1971) and Nunnally (1978) provide good introductions to the topic of validity.

Reliability. The reliability of an instrument refers to the consistency of its measurement. Consistency can occur among items in the same test, between two forms of the same instrument, and between scores on the same instrument given at different times. The corresponding reliability estimates are internal consistency, equivalence, and stability, respectively.

A *reliability coefficient* indicates the proportion of an instrument's variance that is not due to errors of measurement. For example, a reliability coefficient of .90 indicates that 90 percent of the variance of an instrument is nonerror variance or true variance and ten percent is error variance. The reliability coefficient is partly a function of the number of items in the instrument; lengthening an instrument by adding items similar to those already present increases its reliability. An acceptable internal consistency coefficient for an instrument of approximately forty items is .80. If an instrument is shorter than forty items, you can estimate the effect of lengthening this instrument on its reliability by using the Spearman-Brown Formula (Nunnally, 1978, pp. 211-212).

Estimates of reliability coefficients are based on correlation coefficients. The internal consistency estimates depend on the average correlation among items, while the equivalence and stability estimates are correlations between two forms of the instrument and correlations between two different administrations of the same instrument, respectively. Normally, you should use Coefficient Alpha (Nunnally, 1978, pp. 212-215) to obtain internal consistency estimates. Coefficient Alpha is more general than the once widely used split-half method because it is the average of all possible split-half coefficients. If the items are dichotomously scored (for example, right-wrong or true-false), then KR-20 (Nunnally, 1978, p. 214), a special case of Coefficient Alpha, may be used to compute the internal consistency estimate. You should always obtain an internal consistency estimate because, if it is low, the instrument either is too short or lacks homogeneity. If the instrument contains subscales, internal consistency estimates should be obtained for each one. For subscales of fewer than forty items, use the Spearman-Brown Formula. If lack of length rather than lack of homogeneity is contributing to low internal consistency estimates, the estimates from the Spearman-Brown Formula should exceed .80 in most cases. If the instrument or its subscales lack homogeneity, additional work on the items is necessary.

Two special situations, those involving raters and those involving the use of criterion-referenced, domain-referenced, or mastery tests, may require different approaches to estimating reliability. Estimation of the reliability of raters normally involves agreement among different raters, but it may also involve the rating as a reliable indicator of the object being rated. The reliability of criterion-referenced tests can mean either the reliability of the test score or the reliability of the decision based on the test score. Furthermore, since the use of criterion-referenced tests often results in a restriction of the variance of the test, traditional methods of estimating reliability are not always appropriate since such restrictions artificially lower the correlationally based reliability coefficient. More information on estimating the reliability of raters is provided by Frick and Semmel (1979) and Guilford (1954). For information on estimating the reliability of criterion-referenced tests, consult Berk (1980) and Popham (1978).

Traditional reliability estimates are being replaced more and more often in behavioral science research by coefficients of generalizability. Generalizability theory has been proposed by Cronbach and his associates (Cronbach and others, 1972) as an extension of classical reliability theory. According to them, internal consistency reliability estimates are special cases of coefficients of generalizability. For a given test, internal consistency estimates are conceived as static characteristics, whereas coefficients of generalizability vary according to when the test is given, under what conditions, and to whom. Brennan (1983) provides an excellent introduction to generalizability theory.

Locating and Developing Instruments. Normally you should use existing instrumentation in your study. See the last section of Chapter Three for suggested sources of appropriate instrumentation. In addition, check with your dissertation director and other members of your committee for suggestions about instruments. Instruments cited in journal articles, convention papers, and dissertations, if not already widely available, can usually be obtained by contacting the author of the article or paper.

Using existing instrumentation has several advantages. First, you will save considerable time by not having to develop your own instrument. Second, you probably will be able to find sufficient reliability and validity data to permit evaluation of the instrument's appropriateness and to make easier your defense of the instrument before your committee. Third, your results can be compared to those of others who have used the same instruments.

If you cannot locate appropriate instrumentation, you will need to develop your own. Instrument development is time-consuming and requires field testing and careful analysis of the results before you can use the instrument in your study. Despite the work involved, however, it is better to develop your own instrument than to use an existing instrument that is not entirely appropriate for your purpose.

The development of an instrument generally follows the process outlined below. Consult textbooks on psychometric theory (Nunnally, 1978) or test construction (Gronlund, 1982) for a more detailed explanation.

1. *Domain definition:* Operationally define the trait of interest, construct a set of objectives, or otherwise describe the characteristics of the particular situation, object, or event that you wish to measure.

2. *Item pool:* Develop a set of potential items (questions) containing more items than you intend to use.

3. *Content validity:* Check the content validity of your item pool by having subject-matter experts rate the appropriateness of the items.

4. *One-to-one administration:* Administer the items to a few individuals representative of the population for which the instrument is intended. Discuss the items with each individual after he or she has completed the instrument to check for any problem with wording, time, directions, or level of difficulty. Make any necessary revisions.

5. *Field test:* Administer the items to a large representative group. Perform an item analysis and, if subscales are presumed, a factor analysis. Item analysis statistics are based on large sample theory; however, in most cases a sample of thirty individuals will be sufficient. If you are able to get a sample of 300 to 400, then do so, but you probably will have to settle for a much smaller number.

6. *Analysis:* The statistics normally needed for an item analysis are a measure of item difficulty and variability, a measure of the item's ability to discriminate between high and low scorers on the instrument, and an estimate of the internal consistency and reliability of the instrument. Item difficulty and variability are usually estimated by the mean and standard deviation of the item. A common method of determining the item's discrimination is to correlate the item with the total score. This correlation is called an item-total correlation. If subscales are presumed, the correlation of the item with the subscale total should also be calculated. Factor analysis is used to confirm your presumed subscale structure. This analysis will be rather unstable for small samples, so its results should be viewed as indicative rather than definitive. An elementary introduction to factor analysis is provided by Guertin and Bailey (1970). A computer will make the conduct of both the item analysis and the factor analysis much easier. If you have access to the Statistical Package for the Social Sciences (SPSS), use the RELIABILITY procedure for the item analysis and the FACTOR procedure for the factor analysis.

7. *Revisions:* Items should be retained, modified, or deleted based on the results of the item analysis. A key indicator is the item-total correlation. Items with item-total correlations above .30 are functioning well, but items with item-total correlations between .10 and .30 should be examined for possible revisions. Items with item-total correlations less than .10, especially those with negative values, should be deleted or substantially modified. (Note: These guidelines for item retention do not apply to criterion-referenced or mastery tests. For further information see Popham (1978).)

8. *Finalization of instrument:* Perform additional field testing as necessary until you have an instrument with a sufficient number of items, all having satisfactory item-total correlations, and with a sufficient level of reliability.

9. *Other reliability and validity estimates:* If other reliability or validity estimates are needed, you will have to obtain these in a subsequent pilot study.

Materials, Tasks, and Treatments

Depending on the nature of your study, separate sections dealing with materials, tasks, and treatment conditions may be required in your proposal. In the section on materials, describe any required materials, apparatus, or equipment that has not been described previously. Give a complete description if the materials are unfamiliar or used in an unusual way. Examples of materials that would require description are instructional materials, advance organizers, a schematic diagram of a village used in an anthropological study on tribal property, and materials developed for parent education. Equipment that might require special description includes polygraphs, electrocardiographs, special timers, and/or monitoring devices.

The section on tasks should describe completely any that are unique or complex enough to make a simple description insufficient. Ordinarily, tasks are not independent or dependent variables but rather are the media through which the treatment is delivered. However, complete understanding of the treatment and often of the other variables in the study, especially the dependent variables, will depend on understanding of the tasks.

In the section on treatment, describe your experimental settings and particular treatment conditions very carefully. This information makes understanding and evaluation of your treatment easier and enables others to replicate your research. Your description should emphasize the similarities and differences between treatment conditions so that it is clear how each condition compares to each other condition.

Pilot Study

The results of a pilot study provide guidance for shaping the main study. Purposes of a pilot study may include determining the feasibility of proposed research procedures, examining the reasonableness of assumptions, performing a preliminary test of hypotheses, determining the appropriateness of measurement instruments (including field testing of newly developed or newly revised instruments), and estimating the effect size so that an appropriate sample size can be determined for the main study. Results of a pilot study may produce procedural changes, improved measurement, more appropriate dependent measures, more confidence in assumptions, and a better design for the main study. In addition, the results of a pilot study may cause modifications in existing hypotheses and proposals of new hypotheses. In rare cases the results may indicate design difficulties so serious that the main study must be abandoned.

In most cases you will conduct your pilot study before you complete your proposal. That way, you can modify the main study's design and rationale based on the results of the pilot study. If you do this, include the results of the pilot study in your proposal, either in a special section or in an appendix.

A pilot study often is a miniature of the main study, though a pilot study designed to field test an instrument or determine the reliability of raters ordinarily will not replicate all the conditions in the main study. The sample used for the pilot study must be representative of the sample intended for the main study, but no individual who participates in the pilot study should be included in the sample for the main study.

The number of individuals used in a pilot study may be limited by the accessibility of an appropriate sample or by the researcher's desire to complete this phase of the research fairly quickly. Probably thirty or more individuals would be desirable to field test an instrument, while estimating the reliability of raters may require only five or six raters. The number needed to conduct a miniature of the main study would depend upon the number of groups required. If you plan to conduct a pilot study, you should provide some rationale for the size of the sample you decide to use.

Sometimes a pilot study is proposed in the proposal rather than conducted ahead of time. This often occurs if the purpose of the pilot study is to field test an instrument or to examine a specific aspect of the main study's design. In these situations your discussion should anticipate plausible resolutions of the issue being examined and outline how you intend to proceed with the main study if certain contingencies or difficulties occur as a result of the pilot study.

Procedures

In the procedures section of your proposal, describe precisely how you intend to conduct your study. This section should be complete enough so that the procedures could be replicated by another researcher. Indicate what steps will be taken prior to, during, and after data collection. Preparations that may be necessary before collecting data include developing materials, obtaining or constructing equipment, obtaining permission for subjects to participate, constructing questionnaires or other instruments, training raters or other experimenters, and conducting a pilot study. For the actual data collection, describe how you will involve the subjects, what they will be asked to do, how much time will be involved, and how you will actually obtain the data. If a treatment is involved, describe how the treatment will be applied. In addition, you should indicate how you intend to conform to the principles governing research with human subjects as formulated by the American Psychological Association (1982) or other professional organizations. Finally, describe how the subjects will be debriefed and what arrangement, if any, will be made for providing feedback to the subjects.

Design and Data Analysis

This section of your proposal should describe the statistical design associated with your research design and the statistical procedures you propose to use for data analysis. Your committee will need detailed knowledge of your design and procedures in order to properly evaluate their appropriateness and your ability to execute them. Other researchers who wish to replicate your design and analysis will also benefit from a complete description. Last but not least, a carefully prepared set of procedures will provide invaluable guidance to you when you actually analyze your data.

A schematic diagram accompanied by a written narrative is usually the best way to present your statistical design and show the relationship of particular statistical procedures to it. For example, numbering the groups in a 3 x 4 x 2 analysis of variance design facilitates the specification of group contrasts, especially interaction contrasts, and the discussion of subsequent analyses. A schematic representation of a structural model or path model is virtually essential to the understanding of the model. When a schematic representation of a design is not possible, the written explanation should be very detailed.

Presentation of statistical procedures should include, at a minimum, the name or description of each procedure, the dependent and independent variables, the level of significance, and the hypotheses and research questions being addressed by the procedure. If the procedure is commonly employed by other researchers in the field, its name is sufficient. A reference and, perhaps, a formula should be supplied for established procedures that are not commonly employed by other researchers. If you propose a strategy that is unnamed or associated with only a few previous studies, provide a complete description along with any existing references.

Certain other information is needed for some procedures. For procedures associated with a statistical model, specification of the model will clarify the proposed analysis. Models are most often specified for analysis of variance, analysis of covariance, path analysis, and regression analysis. You can describe your model verbally or present it as an equation. For example, a verbal description of an analysis of covariance model might be: a 3 (conditions) x 2 (sex) analysis of covariance with the post-test achievement score as the dependent variable and the pretest achievement score as the covariate. An example of a regression model expressed as an equation is:

$Y = b_0; b_1 X_1 + b_2 X_2 + e$, where Y is the score on the dependent variable;
X_1 is the score on the self-concept measure;
X_2 is the score on the locus of control measure;
e represents the individual's random error score; and
b_0, b_1, b_2 are estimates of the regression coefficients.

All statistical procedures are based on assumptions. Some assumptions can be violated without seriously affecting the procedure, while violation of others will interfere with the proper interpretation of the procedure's results. You should identify the assumptions behind the procedures you have chosen and indicate how you intend to examine their reasonableness. Examples of critical assumptions include homogeneity of regression in the analysis of covariance, homogeneity of variance in the analysis of variance when group sizes are unequal, homogeneity of covariance in a repeated measures design, and independence of continuous and group membership predictors in a regression analysis. Violations of these assumptions have serious consequences and would require a change in your analytic strategy.

Analytic options should be specified for those procedures that require them or that have critical assumptions that may be violated. Examples of options are the determination of the order of entry of predictor variables into a regression analysis, strategy to employ if the correlations among predictors in a regression equation exceed a certain level, and alternative strategies made necessary by violations of critical assumptions, such as using a Johnson-Neyman (Pedhazur, 1982) procedure if continuous and group membership variables interact in a regression analysis.

Describe any subsequent analyses you plan to perform in the event that you find significant results when comparing several means or proportions using the analysis of variance or chi-square analysis, respectively. Ordinarily these subsequent analyses provide some protection against the probability of a Type I error increasing when many comparisons are made; for this reason, they are called simultaneous inference procedures. The most common simultaneous inference procedures are those of Scheffe (S-method), Tukey (T-method), Newman and Keuls (multiple range test), Duncan (new multiple range test), and Dunn (Bonferroni t-statistics). Consult Miller (1981) for a complete treatment of these and other simultaneous inference procedures, and Winer (1971), Kirk (1982), and Marascuilo (1971) for examples of their use in the behavioral sciences.

You should also present the results of any analysis of the power of the statistical procedures you have conducted to determine sample size. Including these results along with the sample sizes required for alternative values of power will permit proper evaluation of the proposed sample size.

The appropriateness of a given statistical procedure for your study should depend on the procedure's ability to address your research questions, not on its complexity. Your graduate training should have made you aware of procedures that are widely used in your field and shown you where to find information about them. Ideally, you should be prepared to deal competently with a wide range of statistical procedures. A treatment of specific statistical procedures is beyond the scope of this book, but Appendix B contains a selected bibligraphy of the statistical procedures most used by behavioral scientists. Some familiarity with the sources listed there is strongly recommended.

Summary

The method chapter of your proposal contains a detailed description of your research design—the plan and structure of your study. It is the blueprint that will guide you when you perform your study. Chapter Six provided specific guidance for preparing your method chapter.

Your method chapter should begin with a description of your population and sample, including the kind of sampling procedures you plan to use. The sample chosen should have both representativeness and independence of units and should be large enough to minimize sampling error and provide adequate power for whatever statistical procedure you intend to use for data analysis.

The instruments section of your method chapter should describe the measurement instruments or procedures you plan to use to provide the data for your study. The instruments or procedures you choose should be both valid and reliable. Use existing instruments if possible. If you cannot find instruments that meet your needs, you can develop your own instruments by following our suggested procedures.

Depending on the nature of your study, separate sections dealing with materials, tasks, and treatment conditions may be required in your proposal. You may also need to conduct a pilot study and report its results or else suggest such a study in the proposal. The method chapter of your proposal will also contain sections describing the procedures you intend to use and the research design and statistical methods you plan to employ in data analysis.

The next chapter describes the process of defending a proposal and presents suggestions to help ensure a successful defense.

 SEVEN

Defending and Refining the Proposal

Brian hated speaking in public, and he didn't consider himself a brilliant researcher, either. Thus it wasn't surprising that his upcoming proposal defense terrified him. He was determined, however, to get through the ordeal as best he could. He carefully followed all his university's rules about deadlines, signatures, and paperwork. He talked to his director and other students about defenses and even attended a friend's defense in the hope that seeing one would lessen his fear. He scheduled his own defense early in the semester "to get it over with." He worked long hours to prepare a clear proposal abstract and practiced his oral summary over and over. He arrived at his defense dressed neatly and on time, though his hands were trembling. He stuttered as he began his summary, but then practice began to tell and he became more confident. Although his committee decided that he needed to make minor revisions before his proposal could be fully approved, Brian was happy. "It wasn't as bad as I thought," he said afterward. "I mean, they might have made me go through another defense!"

Kenny, on the other hand, spoke easily whether in public or in private. In fact, he'd often counted on his charm as well as his quick mind to get him out of tight spots. He knew his study could be an important one, so he hadn't felt it necessary to worry much about details. A missed signature on some paperwork delayed his proposal hearing until May, but Kenny didn't care. He felt that the hearing was just a formality, anyway, since he knew that his director approved of his topic. Kenny arrived at his hearing late, dressed in casual attire. He launched into a witty but rambling summary that lasted half an hour and said more about how original and significant his work was than about what, exactly, he proposed to do. When the question-and-answer period finally began, one committee member began an increasingly critical line of questioning that pointed up a major flaw in Kenny's research plan. Unable to find good answers to the criticism, Kenny lost his charm and became defensive and belligerent. His committee passed him with requirements for major revisions, and his director told him later that he had come close to failing.

Most universities require some kind of official hearing during which a student defends his or her dissertation proposal before a faculty committee. The format, formality, and rigor of such hearings vary widely from school to school, however. If your school does not require a formal proposal defense, you should at least suggest meeting with your committee to discuss your proposal thoroughly before you make a final commitment to carrying out your study. Preparing for a proposal defense, either formal or informal, is an excellent way to prepare yourself to actually do your research and write your dissertation. Most students who successfully pass a proposal defense also finish their dissertations.

When considering whether it is time for you to begin the process of scheduling a proposal defense, ask yourself these three questions:

- Do you have the approval of your director and committee members to proceed?
- Does your proposal meet the minimum requirements of your department and university?
- Do you believe that you can actually carry out the study you are proposing?

If you can answer yes to all three questions, you are ready.

Preparing for Your Defense

Find out from your director or department clerk as early as possible exactly how proposal defenses are scheduled at your school and what paperwork is involved. Begin the process of filing necessary papers early in the semester during which you hope to have your proposal defense. Keep in close touch with the department clerk responsible for the filing. Make sure that you obtain necessary signatures, submit materials in correct form, and meet all deadlines, since failure to do any of these things can sometimes cause months of delay, as Kenny in our opening example found out. Do not ask for changes in deadlines except in cases of major emergency such as a serious illness.

Submit a final copy of your proposal to your committee at the time you file your request for scheduling of a defense. Proposal defenses usually must be scheduled several weeks in advance of the defense date, so expect your defense to be held at least three weeks after the date you file your request.

Many students decide they are ready for their defenses only in the last month of the semester. Then they rush to get papers filed, defense dates assigned, and defenses completed before faculty disappear for Christmas or summer vacations. Not surprisingly, defense dates become hard to get at these times, especially in the case of spring semester. The wise student will therefore make every effort to schedule his or her defense early in the semester. You are likely to get a more relaxed hearing in October or March than you will in December or May.

One good way of preparing yourself for your proposal defense is to seek out other students who have just completed the proposal process, preferably under your dissertation director, and discuss their experiences with them. Attend a proposal defense, if these are open to students. Discuss with your director the ground rules by which your defense will be conducted. You should also ask your director to take notes of the committee's suggestions during your defense.

Even if your department does not require you to submit a proposal abstract before the day of your defense, you would be well advised to prepare one. Make sure that this terse yet comprehensive review of your proposal is well written, because it is likely to be the first part of your written work that your examiners see.

Defending Your Proposal

Proposal defenses used to be less complex and formal than they often are today, and proposals were simply accepted or rejected. Nowadays, however, proposal defenses are viewed as developmental experiences for students, and a category of conditional approval has come into use. Proposals may be either accepted as they stand or accepted with conditions demanding major or minor revisions. These conditions are more or less formally spelled out, and the topic and proposal are finally approved only when the student satisfactorily completes the specified conditions. Occasionally, proposals are rejected entirely at a proposal defense.

You, too, should try to view your proposal defense in a developmental light. Be prepared to accept a conditional approval as a mark of satisfactory work completed. If you put yourself in this frame of mind, you will feel less threatened by criticism and more likely to ask for and/or accept suggestions for improving your proposal.

Enter your proposal defense assuming that the examining committee is on your side. A relaxed frame of mind will communicate your positive expectation to your examiners. At the same time, make certain that you, your abstract, and your proposal show well. Arrive on time and well dressed. Make sure, too, that the printed copies of your abstract and proposal are professionally prepared. Poorly typed material, full of spelling errors and bad grammar, is likely to be seen as the mark of an imprecise researcher.

Your proposal hearing will most likely begin with your presentation of a short oral summary of the proposal. This summary normally should last about fifteen minutes. The oral presentation gives the examining committee a chance to recall the proposal and determine how well acquainted you are with it. A confident, well-organized oral summary is bound to make a good first impression on your examiners.

Make yourself as comfortable as possible during your

summary and examination. If you find the room too warm or cold, adjust the heat. Provide yourself with a glass of water. If you talk with more authority on your feet, ask permission to stand up to deliver your summary. If you find that you can make your points more forcefully by using a blackboard, arrange ahead of time to have one available in the examining room. Should you find yourself breaking out in a cold sweat or stuttering, like Brian in our opening example, stop the action for a moment while you take a few deep breaths and maybe a sip of water. It is better to look a little nervous but in control than to make major errors because of your tension.

Much of the time in a proposal defense will be spent in questions and answers. Make certain that you understand the questions your examiners ask before you attempt to answer them; then answer them precisely. It often helps to give an accurate paraphrase of each question before you answer. If you find you do not understand an examiner's question, ask that it be repeated or rephrased. You might also ask your director to help rephrase a question you have trouble understanding.

If you find that a line of questioning seems to be uncovering a weakness in your proposal, don't be afraid to volunteer a possible adjustment to your design or ask for advice on ways to improve the proposal. Remember, you want to walk out of your defense with an approved topic, even if conditions for revision are attached. If neither you nor your examiners are able to think of a solution to a newly discovered problem now, you may find a solution later.

On the other hand, if you believe your design is correct and the examiner is simply pressing for a modification to suit his or her own point of view, defend your design. Remember that you have spent much more time considering and developing your proposal than your examiners have spent reading it. Don't be belligerent in the process, however. Often it will prove to be most prudent to accept the suggestion, move on, and consider the matter again later.

Revising Your Proposal

If your proposal is passed with conditions, do not be distressed. Instead, try to make the required additions, amendments, or deletions as soon as possible. If your committee passes on the changes required in the form of a memorandum or if your director took good notes during your defense, your task will be much easier. When examiners rely on their memories to reconstruct the issues they wanted corrected or when some suggestions made during the proposal defense were more in the nature of musings than requirements, confusion can easily occur. For this reason, it is very important that you and your director write out, immediately after the defense, a clear description of the changes to be made.

You may find that you need to make further revisions in your proposal even after it has been approved, due to unforeseen events that occur as you conduct your study. Minor revisions are usually permissible, even expected; but major revisions are likely to need special approval. Some schools even insist that the final report not deviate from the proposal. Some of the most useful discoveries in research have come from fortuitous observations made during a study and capitalized on by the researcher, however, and most schools recognize that any regulations limiting your opportunity to do some adjusting of your plans interferes with creative research. A major job of your research committee is to help you enrich your research by insights produced in the later stages of the process, so they are likely to approve beneficial adjustments you make in your plans while conducting your study.

Normally, changes made while conducting the study are not translated into formal revisions of your proposal, although you may find it useful to make penciled changes on a working copy. Only if changes are very significant might you wish to write a letter to your committee that explains how the changes differ from the original proposal and asks their approval of the changes in writing.

The Security of an Approved Topic

An approved dissertation proposal is a type of contract between the student and the university. The contract may be limited to a three- or five-year period during which the dissertation is to be completed, but it is generally assumed that the university will consider the topic acceptable during whatever period is allowed, even if the director leaves or the committee changes before the student completes the final report.

Very little testing has been done in the courts of the implications of approved proposals as contracts binding universities. But it is probable that your university could not renege on its acceptance of your proposed topic and would be obligated to make reasonable efforts to see you through to the completion of your study within the time frame allotted you, despite the departure of your entire committee or the collapse of your program or even the disbanding of your department.

The implication of the accepted proposal as a contract is one reason for suggesting that you set up your own proposal defense, even if it is not required by your department, and try to make sure that the department chairperson attends the defense.

Once you have passed your proposal defense and complied with all conditions, by all means celebrate. You deserve it! Believe it or not, you are now more than halfway through the dissertation process. But limit your celebration to an evening or a weekend, then get back to work at the beginning of the next week. Let your exhilaration and energy spur you on to complete your project.

Summary

A hearing or defense is usually required before a student receives final approval for a dissertation proposal. This hearing provides a formal arena in which the student explains his or her research topic and design and answers questions about it. If your school does not require a formal proposal defense, you will benefit by scheduling an informal one yourself. Whether the defense is formal or informal, you should prepare for it carefully.

Begin by finding out your department's requirements for scheduling, format, and paperwork; then follow them to the letter. Obtain all necessary signatures and meet all deadlines. Find out what goes on during a proposal defense by talking with your director and with other students who have been through the process. Allow plenty of time for scheduling your defense, and try to have the defense take place fairly early in the semester. Write a well-organized abstract of your proposal to present at your defense.

Arrive at your proposal defense on time, neatly dressed, and with a positive attitude. The defense will most likely begin with a fifteen-minute oral summary of your work. Present this summary as calmly and confidently as you can. During the rest of your defense, do your best to answer the questions put to you. Don't be afraid of criticism, but stand your ground if you feel you have been criticized unfairly.

Look on your proposal defense as a developmental experience. Naturally you will hope for complete approval, but don't be ashamed if your proposal is approved conditionally with a request for revisions. Discuss the revisions with your director as soon as possible after the hearing to make sure you understand what is required. Then make the revisions promptly. You may need your committee's approval to make other major revisions after your study begins, but this should not be necessary for minor changes of plan.

An approved dissertation proposal is a kind of contract between you and the university. Enjoy the security that it represents, but use your enthusiasm as a spur to help you complete your dissertation.

As you begin your actual study, you may find that you need one or more types of professional assistance. The next chapter gives you some tips on using computers, consultants, and other aids to make your study more accurate and complete.

 EIGHT

Using Computers
and Other Sources
of Research Assistance

Bijan, an Iranian student doing graduate work
at an American university, wanted to make his dissertation a statistical study on changes in the population of several racial groups in certain major cities
of Iran during the last twenty years. He felt handicapped, however, both by his limited knowledge of
English and by his inability to acquire the relevant
statistics without returning to Iran, which he could
not do for political reasons.

Following some leads he found in the Smithsonian Institution's *Scholars' Guide to Washington,
D.C., for Middle Eastern Studies,* Bijan found some
of the statistics he needed in the collections of special libraries devoted to the Middle East. A librarian in one of those libraries in turn directed him to
an official of an oil company that had, for its own
reasons, conducted population studies in Iran, and
he was able to obtain the company's research data
as well. After making some modifications in his research plan to focus on the data he had been able
to obtain, Bijan proceeded with his study.

Bijan did the simpler of his analyses on his
roommate's microcomputer, using a popular statistical package. He used the computer as a word processor for typing his dissertation as well. Some of
the analyses he needed could not be handled by

111

the small computer, however, so Bijan learned how to interface his roommate's system with the university's mainframe. The more complete statistical packages available on the larger computer gave Bijan everything he needed. He studied the software manuals carefully to learn how the programs worked and how data should be entered, and he checked some of the computer-produced analyses by hand.

As a finishing touch, before submitting his dissertation manuscript, Bijan hired an editor to go over it and correct his mistakes in English. "Your statistical work is brilliant, and your writing is very competent, too," his director told him later.

Preparing a dissertation is often a long and arduous process, and you should take advantage of all the legitimate help you can get. Naturally, the full responsibility for doing the research involved in your study and writing the dissertation describing that research is still yours, and you must not abdicate even a small part of it to anyone else. However, you can quite properly call on consultants to advise you in certain ways, and you can use a computer to save yourself many hours of tedium and trouble in analyzing and interpreting data and in typing drafts of your dissertation.

This chapter covers a number of professional aids, most notably the computer, that you can use while doing research and preparing your dissertation. It includes consultants such as editors, content specialists, and computer consultants. The chapter describes how each of these things and people can help you and tells how and when that aid may ethically be used. It also discusses other matters of ethics you will need to consider during your study, such as those involving use of human and animal experimental subjects and those involving quotation of other writers' material.

The Computer

Quite possibly you have already learned how to use a computer during your graduate studies or before. If you have not, we strongly recommend doing so as soon as possible. Take advantage of workshops, short classes, or individual consultations offered by your university computer center or other sources.

Learning how to use a computer does take practice, so be prepared to set aside time for it. The benefits will be well worth the effort you invest. Computers are so much a part of behavioral science research today that almost any study can benefit from their use.

Many students today own microcomputers and have found them invaluable in their work. If you don't have your own micro, see if you can borrow one or use one belonging to a friend or colleague. A visit to a good computer store can give you an idea of the kinds of available software that are compatible with a given machine and that might be useful for your study.

If you can't get access to a microcomputer, or if your analyses require a larger computer, investigate the services of your university computer center. The use of a university computer for your dissertation will rarely cost you anything. Most schools provide graduate students with a special account for dissertation research. While the account ordinarily has a specific dollar limit, you can usually get additional funds if necessary. Check with your director or your computer center for details on applying for a computer account.

Why Use a Computer? Chapter Three told you how to use computer data bases for making literature searches, but that's just one of the many ways a computer can be helpful in your research. Your university computer center is likely to have software that can perform a wide variety of statistical analyses with amazing speed and accuracy. Software for some of these analyses is available for microcomputers as well. You can also use a microcomputer or a terminal connected to a larger computer for word processing as you write your dissertation.

A computer can be particularly helpful when you are analyzing and interpreting data, especially if your study involves complex calculations or large amounts of information. Kerlinger (1979) gives a graphic example of the time saved by using a computer to perform a relatively straightforward analysis. To do a factor analysis of a twenty-item attitude scale in 1958, Kerlinger and an associate first calculated the 190 correlation coefficients needed on a mechanical desk calculator, a job that took many hours. Then they paid about $600 to have a factor analysis, without rotations, performed using a primitive computer. Finally they spent twenty hours doing the rotations by hand. Kerlinger reports that a similar analysis took less than twenty seconds on a computer of the late 1970s. Today, computers are even faster—and, perhaps more important, they are available to a much larger number of students.

Because of its accuracy, a computer is ideal even for simple calculations such as means, standard deviations, and correlation coefficients. Students are particularly likely to make mistakes in routine calculations in behavioral science research because these calculations are so boring—especially when there are a lot of them. A computer, however, never becomes bored or sleepy. If you enter the correct data in the proper format and are using the right software, your results should be accurate every time. Software for doing most simple statistical analyses is available for microcomputers as well as through university computer systems.

Major statistical software packages (discussed later in this chapter) provide the well-documented output you will need for proper interpretation of your analysis. In addition to the results of the particular analysis requested, the output usually contains associated descriptive statistics that can be very helpful in interpreting these results. The output also has the exact probability value for any significance tests involved, which helps you determine whether a result is significant. The output from some analyses contains summary data needed for further analyses, such as constructing confidence intervals or comparing several means.

The graphics capability of today's computers can also help you in data interpretation. When used with appropriate software and a graphics-capable printer, a microcomputer can usually produce simple charts. In addition, most large statistical packages can provide visual displays of more complex things, such as frequency distributions of variables, scatter plots of the relationship between two variables, residuals in regression analysis, clusters of variables in factor analysis and principal components analysis, or groupings of stimuli or individuals in cluster analysis. By using plotters, available in the computer centers of most universities, you can obtain graphs of lines and curves, topological contour maps showing areas of varying densities, or specialized plots particular to the needs of your study. Be warned, however, that while graphs from statistical packages are easily obtained, the plotter usually requires a special program to be written. If you are not able to write such programs, you will have to seek help from an experienced programmer.

In addition to showing the results of analyses graphically, the computer can help you conduct graphic analyses. Since the publication of *Exploratory Data Analysis* (Tukey, 1977), a spate of useful graphic methods has appeared in the literature (Wainer and Thissen, 1981). Tukey presented a rationale for these methods when he stated that a good graph "forces us to notice what we never expected to see" (p. vi). Many of these graphic analyses would be difficult to do without a computer.

Using a computer as a word processor can greatly aid you in preparing written materials for your study as well as your dissertation manuscript itself. A word processor allows you to add, delete, or move large or small pieces of text easily, without retyping. It makes formatting and insertion of tables and figures easy. Special kinds of word processing software can format footnotes, check your spelling, or index your manuscript. In addition, new "idea processing" software can help you outline and organize your thoughts at any stage of your study. Some integrated software packages allow you to move data between an "electronic card file," your manuscript, and graphs. When done on a letter-quality printer (not, unfortunately, the same kind of printer that can produce graphics, which is usually a dot matrix printer), the output of a word processor resembles the output of a good electric typewriter.

A wide variety of word processing software and related programs (such as spelling checkers) are now available for microcomputers, and if you own a micro or can borrow one, you will very likely want to do your word processing on that machine. You can also probably do word processing on a terminal connected to your university's multiuser computer system, but response time may be slow if many people are using the system. This means that what you type will not appear immediately on the terminal screen, which can be disorienting. You also may have to go to a special building or area to pick up your printed ("hard copy") output.

If you have a microcomputer, consult with your university computer center about the possibility of interfacing your micro with their larger system. If this can be done, you may be able to send selected data from your computer to theirs whenever you need complex analyses or "number crunching" that your small machine can't handle.

The computer's interactive capability can be a great help with activities such as data collection and the presentation of your treatment. Using interactive software, a computer can present material to people at other terminals and record their responses. A computer can even be used to manage an experiment. For example, McLaughlin (1981) used a computer to teach programming to subjects in his dissertation study. A computer presented the treatment, consisting of either a discovery or didactic instructional strategy. It provided feedback to the subjects according to the conditions of their treatment group. Finally, using a special program, it recorded and stored information regarding the number and type of transactions (entries) that each individual made, the amount of time between each transaction, and the responses of each individual to the test items administered via the terminal and to requests for demographic information.

Another form of interaction, the computer simulation, can help you in building models and formulating hypotheses. You can use known data to design a simulation and then use the simulation to discover the effect that changing a certain variable will have on a variety of other variables. You probably will need to know programming in order to explore this use of the computer.

Finally, the computer can help you with activities such as sampling and scoring of instruments. It can provide you with a set of random numbers to use in lieu of a printed table of random numbers for selecting a sample, or it can actually sample cases from a preexisting large data set. You can score individual protocols (answer sheets) after data are stored in the computer by writing scoring programs or by using existing programs. Scoring in this way allows you to experiment with various scoring procedures. In addition, mark-sensitive cards or sheets on which individuals have recorded responses can be read by optical scoring machines. In many cases, the resulting data can be placed directly onto magnetic tape or discs for computer analysis.

Caveats. Computers can be wonderful—but only if used in the right way. If you plan to use computers in your study, you should keep several important warnings in mind.

First and foremost: always, always, ALWAYS make a backup of your work. You should probably have both a hard copy (printed) and a tape or disc backup for anything that is important. Computers are not perfect, and things do happen to them and to material stored on them. Loss of data can be a nuisance or a disaster, depending on the data, but it's never something you want to risk happening. For that matter, you should make backups even if you don't use a computer. Photocopy your dissertation manuscript and other important written material and keep the copy in a different location from the original. This can protect you from the tragedy that might occur if, say, a briefcase containing the only copy of your manuscript or important data were lost or stolen.

Second, be aware of the possibility that your computer files may be seen by unauthorized eyes. Spying and tampering in computer centers is rare, but not as rare as it used to be or ought to be. This is a particularly important matter when the privacy of your subjects is involved. To protect that privacy from possible violation, don't identify your subjects by name in information stored on a computer. Use codes for identification instead.

Third, don't expect the computer to be a substitute for skill in data analysis. Avoid the temptation to use an analytical procedure you don't really understand simply because it is available in a statistical package. This can result in inappropriate, unnecessary, or confusing analyses. Always use the computer in a planned way.

If you use statistical packages, don't abdicate your responsibility to make critical decisions about analytic options. When options are available, the program ordinarily contains a default value or strategy that a user must consciously override in situations when it is not appropriate. By automatically using the default options, you allow the person who wrote the statistical program to decide what is best for your analysis.

For example, in a factor analysis you typically want to rotate factors to facilitate interpretation of them. A program for such an analysis will use some convention, specified in the manual for that particular package, to determine the number of factors to rotate from the unrotated solution. In some cases your interpretation of the results from the factor analysis would improve if a larger or smaller number of factors were rotated. By uncritically allowing the program to dictate the options, you allow the computer to "do your thinking for you." Other examples in which failure to exercise your options in an analysis may constrain your interpretation of the findings include the following:

- deciding on the order in which to enter variables into a regression equation (should you use a forward, backward, or stepwise solution, or should you specify a certain order?);
- choosing a simultaneous inference procedure for exploring group differences following an analysis of variance (many such analyses exist);
- choosing a test statistic for a multivariate analysis of variance (there are four major ones and several minor ones); and
- deciding when to terminate an iterative analysis (iterations are involved in many statistical procedures).

Whenever you use a statistical package, you need to determine what options are appropriate for your analysis and to be sure to override any default options that are not appropriate.

Fourth, don't take the computer's word for everything. The usual accuracy and reliability of the computer can lull you into a false sense of security about its output. Many kinds of problems and errors can result in incorrect output. Therefore, examine all output carefully to determine its plausibility. Descriptive statistics often provide clues for detecting problems that may have occurred, so check these statistics carefully. For example, by examining the minimum and maximum values on the output, you may find that values not in the range of the data have been analyzed. This can result either from incorrect data entry or a format problem. Careful entering of the data and verification of the format of the data will help you to avoid such an error.

Incorrect computer output can have many causes. One of the most common is mistakes in transcribing the data and preparing them for entry into the computer ("garbage in, garbage out"). Another is improper data format or incorrect specification of the format in the program. Problems can also occur in the execution of a program, such as attempting to invert a matrix whose determinant is zero (which is analogous to dividing by zero). Often the program will provide error messages concerning certain problems on the output; in other cases, the program will simply terminate or "crash" if certain problems occur.

Finally, don't let the computer's avilability and speed tempt you to forego a personal familiarization with your data. This familiarization is best accomplished by closely examining the data and doing some simple analyses by hand. Once you know your data well, you can let the computer help you enhance your understanding of it.

Programs and Packages. A program is a set of instructions to the computer written in a language that the computer understands. Some examples of programming languages are BASIC, FORTRAN, APL, COBOL, PILOT, PASCAL, and SNOBOL. Writing a computer program requires both the knowledge of a programming language and a logical analysis of the steps involved to produce the desired output, starting from the entry of the data.

Programs are currently available for a large range of statistical analyses. Many of these programs are part of widely available statistical packages, often called library programs or "canned" programs. Whenever possible, use library programs rather than attempting to write your own program. You do not need to understand programming or programming languages in order to use most statistical programs.

The most popular statistical packages are the BMDP series from UCLA (Dixon and Brown, 1983), the SAS systems from North Carolina (Helwig and Council, 1979), and the SPSS system, published by McGraw-Hill Publishing Company (SPSS, Inc., 1983). Subsets of some of these packages are also available for microcomputers. Before buying a statistical package for your micro, make sure it contains the particular analyses you need.

Each statistical package has a manual that describes every program in the system. The description of a program typically includes an overview of the statistical procedures in the program, directions for preparing and entering data, commands needed to execute the program, user options available, examples of output, computational procedures, and references. Once you have selected your data analysis strategy, refer to the manuals to find the proper program. Statistical packages are easy to use and the staff at most computer centers will be glad to provide any help you need.

Preparation of Data. You must prepare your data in certain ways before it can be input into the computer. This preparation includes coding the data in a meaningful way and establishing a uniform format for the data from all subjects. The data must also be transcribed and entered in the form that the computer expects. Common media for data transcription include punched cards, mark-sensitive cards, special mark-sensitive coding sheets for optical scanners, and coding sheets from which the data can be typed directly into the computer through a terminal. Data can be stored on punched cards, magnetic tapes, or disc files for future analysis.

Transcribing the data to an appropriate medium or setting up the format for data to be entered through a terminal takes thought and special planning. First, be sure you identify and collect from your subjects all data that you might need in your study. Most data will fall into one of three categories: demographic data (for example, subject name or ID number, sex, age, race, socioeconomic status, grade in school, years of education, marital status, and/or occupation); data from independent variables, including control and moderator variables, and group membership information; and data from dependent variables. Include all possibly relevant data even if you are uncertain about what you will use. Nothing is so frustrating as later wishing you had obtained certain data from your subjects or that you had coded some information that you did obtain.

Second, code properly all data and other information that will be entered into the computer. A statistical analysis requires numeric data, so you must transform any nonnumeric data intended for a statistical analysis either before entry into the computer or within a program before the execution of the analysis (all statistical packages have provisions for doing this).

No transformation is usually necessary for data already in numeric form. These data probably include the information from your dependent variables and most of your independent variables. However, all nominal data (except those already in numeric form, such as social security numbers or student identification numbers) and any data that will be used for classification in the analysis (for example, ability designations of high, medium, and low) will probably need to be transformed using a numeric code. Most of the demographic data and some of the independent variable data will probably fall into this category. See the manual for the software you are using to find out exactly what kinds of data and formats your program can accept.

The codes that you will use for transformation of nonnumeric to numeric data are arbitrary. Typically, however, consecutive numbers, each having the minimum number of digits necessary, are chosen. When some information is missing, either leave the entry blank or use a special code that you have established for missing values. Whatever coding system you use, be sure to keep a record of all transformations so that you will be able to identify and label your results properly. Some examples of transformations using numeric codes are given in Table 1.

Third, transcribe the data for each subject in your study into a uniform format. The use of 80-column IBM coding sheets makes this task easier. Plan the format carefully before you

Table 1. Examples of Coding Transformations.

Variable	Transformation
Sex	1 = Male
	2 = Female
Treatment	1 = High discovery condition
	2 = Moderate discovery condition
	3 = Low discovery condition
	4 = Didactic control group
	5 = No treatment control group
Education	1 = Below high school
	2 = Some high school
	3 = High school graduate
	4 = Some college
	5 = College graduate (B.A.)
	6 = Professional or graduate training
	7 = Master's degree
	8 = Doctor's degree
IQ	1 = Low (IQ less than 85)
	2 = Medium (IQ between 85 and 115)
	3 = High (IQ greater than 115)
Income	1 = Less than $10,000
	2 = $10,000 - $19,999
	3 = $20,000 - $29,999
	4 = $30,000 - $39,999
	5 = $40,000 or greater

transcribe the data. A master format sheet will serve as your record of the format you chose. A master format sheet lists the columns on the coding sheet in which the code will be entered (if your computer system uses punched cards, these will be the same columns as on the cards), the name of each variable, and the definition of each coding transformation. An example of a master format sheet is given in Table 2.

Other Aids

Guides on Permissions and Ethics. You will likely find that you need a whole array of permissions in order to conduct your study. If you use human subjects, you will need permission

Table 2. Master Format Sheet for a Study.

Column	Variable	Definition of Transformation
1-5	Student ID	5-digit ID number provided by the school
6	Sex	1 = male; 2 = female
7-8	Age	Age of student in years (12-19)
9-10	Grade	Grade in high school (09-12)
11	SES	1 = low; 2 = middle; 3 = high (as previously defined)
12	Treatment	1 = high discovery; 2 = low discovery; 3 = control group
13-15	IQ	3-digit IQ taken from the Stanford Binet Scale
16-17	Pretest	2-digit pretest score
18-19	Locus of Control	2-digit External score on the Rotter Internal-External Locus of Control Scale
20-21	Self-Concept	2-digit score on the Piers-Harris Children's Self-Concept Scale
22-23	Posttest	2-digit posttest score
24-25	Scale 1	2-digit score on the first subscale of the Attitude measure
26-27	Scale 2	2-digit score on the second subscale of the Attitude measure
28-29	Scale 3	2-digit score on the third subscale of the Attitude measure
30-31	Attitude	2-digit total score on the Attitude measure

not only from the subjects themselves (or their parents or guardians, if they are children) but also, in most cases, from a committee in your college or university. If you quote copyrighted material from other authors, you will need permission to do this as well.

If your subjects are children, you should be aware of the provisions of the 1974 Family Educational Rights and Privacy Act (Buckley Amendment) in regard to children as research subjects. Questions concerning use of student records should be addressed to the Family Educational Rights and Privacy Act Office, Department of Education, Washington, D.C.

When you request permission from your campus Committee on Research with Human Subjects, you may need to submit a two- or three-page statement describing the context and nature of your study. This statement should explain how you intend to protect the anonymity of your subjects, reduce or eliminate physical or psychological risk to them, debrief them, and maintain confidentiality of data. Attach a copy of your proposed "informed consent" form, letters of permission already received, and copies of any instruments you are planning to use.

Sometimes your dissertation committee will also act as your committee for research on human subjects. If the two are not the same, however, your proposal must usually be approved by your dissertation committee before the other committee will receive it. Allow yourself enough time to obtain permission from both committees if necessary.

In order to gain permission for your study, you will need to guarantee ethical treatment of your subjects. Ethical research practice simply means humane and considerate ways of interacting with other people, using their productions, and protecting their rights. Such practice is important when dealing with adults and critical when dealing with children. You should familiarize yourself with the principles in the American Psychological Association's *Ethical Principles in the Conduct of Research with Human Participants* (1982) or in similar handbooks published by the U.S. Department of Health and Human Services.

Researchers also must follow a rigid code of ethical treatment when using experimental animals. If you plan to use animals, study the ethical code established by the National Society for Medical Research and the rules set forth in the American Psychological Association's *Principles for the Care and Use of Animals* (1971).

You are responsible for obtaining permission to quote other authors' work in your dissertation. You must abide by the principles of the Copyright Act of 1976 (Title 17 of the United States Code), which provides protection for authors. If you plan to quote or closely paraphrase article or book passages exceeding about fifty words, or to copy graphs, tables, or the like, you should write to the holder of the original copyright and ask for permission to do this. You must also obtain permission to use material appearing in newspapers, magazines, pamphlets, and bulletins. Though U.S. government publications are not copyrighted, it is a good idea to obtain permission to use material from them as well, since these publications sometimes contain previously copyrighted material and the earlier copyright is not nullified because the material appeared in a government publication. If you quote or adapt material from any copyright source, be sure to give credit to the copyright holder in your manuscript.

Organizations and Public Servants. Students are often surprised to learn how much help they can receive from organizations and government agencies. Many organizations have been collecting data for their own purposes for years. These data, often unpublished, can save you hours of time if you know they exist. For example, a student writing a dissertation on day care as a possible preventive of child abuse would be well advised to contact the Day Care Council of America, the Children's Defense Fund, and the National Committee for the Prevention of Child Abuse, to name only a few organizations. Often a simple telephone call can obtain a great deal of data or uncover leads to other sources that have information you need.

Organizations may also become interested enough in your topic to offer volunteer help for your study. Many organizations are glad to aid research that might foster their cause or shed light on their work. Consider these sources as you look for help.

Public employees are usually well informed about issues dealing with their jobs. Employees in the U.S. Bureau of the Census, the U.S. Bureau of Labor Statistics, and the National Center for Education Statistics have proven especially knowledgeable and helpful to behavioral science researchers. Often they have access to data not available to the general public. They may not always be able to respond immediately, but they ordinarily are very cooperative with students doing serious research.

Employees in local government may be able to tell you about sources of assistance previously unknown to you, especially if you arrange to visit them in person. One student, whose topic fit very well with a project being conducted by a division chief in the U.S. Department of Health and Human Services, found that the chief was willing to allow him regular use of a

wide-area telephone service line. The chief benefitted by shar-
ing the information the student obtained, and the student saved
hundreds of dollars in telephone charges.

Consultants. If you need help with some aspect of your
study beyond what the members of your committee can provide, you may want to engage a consultant. The two most common types of consultants for dissertations are statistical consultants and computer consultants. A statistical consultant
might help you with the design of your analysis, the actual
analysis, interpretation of the findings, and presentation of the
findings in your dissertation. A computer consultant might assist you with the preparation of data for input into the computer, the selection of appropriate programs to analyze the
data, and the interpretation of the output. He or she will often
actually execute the program for you. Some consultants handle
both statistical and computer subjects.

Some universities have specific policies regarding the use
of consultants for dissertations. Check with your director concerning any such policy. If you use consultants, either at the
recommendation of your committee or at your own initiation,
remember that the dissertation must remain *your* study. You are
ultimately responsible for its design, its conduct, and its content. Therefore, you should seek consultants who *help* you do
something rather than who do something *for* you.

Choose your consultant carefully. Consultants range from
fellow graduate students who have special knowledge of statistics or statistical packages to university professors, practicing
statisticians, and computer analysts. Be sure to check the cre-
dentials and reputation of any person you contemplate hiring.
Check with your committee or with other students for recommendations. Be sure the statistician you engage understands the
nature of your research and can communicate easily with you.
A computer consultant should have some experience with the
type of data in your study and should be very familiar with the
computer system that you expect to use to process your data.

Work out an agreement with the consultant about fees
and responsibilities before any work is started. Some consultants
charge by the hour, others by the project. Check with other stu-

dents to determine prevailing rates. If a computer consultant charges by the hour and is going to run the program, discuss what happens when the consultant incurs extra time because of his or her own errors.

Keep your committee, especially your director, informed about the help you are receiving. Your committee is responsible for monitoring your progress throughout your study and judging your efforts. Ultimately, each member of the committee must be convinced that you have actually conducted the study and must certify that you have successfully defended it. By keeping your committee informed, you help to make sure that if a committee member has any doubts about the propriety of your consulting help, that member can discuss the problem with you before you complete your analysis. You may want to arrange a meeting between your committee and your consultant to clarify responsibilities and avoid misunderstandings.

Be sure you know exactly what each of your planned analyses entails and what it is intended to accomplish and that you communicate this information accurately to both your committee and your consultant. If your consultant misunderstands your committee's intentions—or yours—concerning a certain analysis, he or she may produce analyses that are inappropriate for your study. Additional analyses will then have to be conducted, often at considerable cost in time and money. Describing your planned analyses in detail in your proposal can help you avoid this problem.

Finally, be sure that you can properly interpret and defend the results from any analysis on which you have had help. The content of your dissertation is your responsibility, and you will have to defend your study at your final oral. Your examiners are bound to ask questions concerning the analysis of the data and your interpretation of the results, and you will need to be able to do more than simply parrot your consultant's words.

Editors and Content Specialists. Naturally, you will want to make the writing in your dissertation—even in its first draft— as clear and correct as possible. Begin your pursuit of this goal by reviewing the suggestions for good writing given in Chapter

One and consulting the references listed there and in Appendix C. Your director and committee will usually offer editorial suggestions on drafts of your dissertation as well. However, no committee member is likely to have the time or the desire to edit your manuscript fully. Therefore, before submitting your final (or perhaps even first) draft to your committee, you may want to hire an editor to review the manuscript.

Since you have been close to your dissertation for so long, you may have lost your objectivity about it. An editor can review the manuscript objectively, looking for problems with overall structure and flow as well as with the structure and syntax of individual sentences. In particular, an editor will look for jargon and slang; hackneyed, extraneous, or vague words and phrases; a folksy or casual writing style; lack of conformity to proper writing style and format; unclear writing; misspelling; and general grammatical problems. An experienced editor can greatly improve the coherence and readability of your manuscript.

You may also want someone who is familiar with the content of your study to review your draft. This person may or may not be the same as the editor. The content expert should review your development of the theoretical framework for your study, your presentation of findings, and your discussion of their implications. This review may detect problems with your presentation that an editor might miss because of lack of knowledge of the content.

If you have trouble with writing and organization, money used to hire an editor, a content specialist, or both will be well spent. A poorly prepared or badly written draft increases review time, makes detection of problems with content more difficult, and is likely to be taken by your committee as evidence of sloppy thinking. On the other hand, a well-edited first draft allows your committee to make a quick, efficient, and thorough review and increases your chances of having to make only minor changes to produce a final draft.

Typists. Before your manuscript is typed, check your university's requirements regarding paper, margins, and the number of copies needed. They will probably specify the size, weight, and fiber content of the paper to be used for the original and for copies; commonly 8½-by-11-inch white bond paper with a twenty pound weight, containing at least 25 percent cotton fiber, is required. Onionskin or erasable paper is usually not permitted because the type on such papers tends to blur with handling. Typically you must submit an original copy of the dissertation and one or more copies, which, in most cases, may be photocopies.

If you have access to a word processor and a letter-quality printer (usually a daisy wheel; copy from a dot matrix printer normally is not acceptable) and are not a terribly slow typist, consider typing your manuscript yourself. You can proofread your work and easily correct any errors before you run your final draft. If you do so, the result will be an extremely clean, perfectly typed manuscript.

If you can't use a word processor, you would probably be wise to hire a typist with experience in dissertation work unless you are an exceptionally good typist. The saving of time and effort and the assurance of a professional-looking manuscript are well worth the expense.

Assistance for Foreign Students. You would be especially well advised to hire an editor and/or consultant if English is not your native language, since your dissertation will have to meet the same criteria for writing style, language precision, and clarity of expression as those of your native English-speaking colleagues. Your campus foreign student office should be able to help you find an acceptable editorial assistant. If you need a language editor or translator, have this person go over your manuscript before you present it to your director. Do not expect either your typist or your director to edit your manuscript.

Many foreign students resist researching a dissertation topic relevant to their home countries because they believe, often rightly, that they will not be able to obtain the resources necessary to do a good job. The ideal solution to this problem is to return home to do the dissertation, but this may not be practical in terms of time and cost. If you plan to attempt a topic related to your home country, make early contact with your embassy, chancellery, or consulate to find out what help is available. You may be able to call on a special staff member who serves as a liaison for foreign students in this country or use a library or information center that gathers and disseminates information on your homeland.

Material about your home country may also be located in special collections in U.S. libraries. Chapter Three listed some publications and directories that can guide you to special collections. You may also find the *Scholars' Guide* series, published by the Smithsonian Institution Press, particularly helpful in this regard, as did Bijan in our opening example. Volumes in this series of area studies guides are available for Latin America and the Caribbean (1979), East Asia (1979), Africa (1980), Central and East Europe (1980), Russia/Soviet Union (1977), South Asia (1981), the Middle East (1981), Northwest Europe (1984), and Southeast Asia (1983). Additional volumes on several other regions of the world are planned. The guides describe the scholarly resources and special collections of the Washington, D.C. area in detail.

Summary

This chapter described a number of people and things that may be helpful to you as you do your research and work on your dissertation. Foremost among these is the computer, which you can use for making literature searches, analyzing and interpreting data, preparing graphic materials, and word processing. The computer may even become an integral part of your experimental study.

You need to use computers correctly if you want them to work effectively for you. Always make backups of your work and protect the confidentiality of your data. Don't expect computer programs to substitute for a thorough familiarity with your data and the appropriate methods of analyzing it. Learn the capabilities of different software packages and choose the one that is right for you. Make sure your input to the computer is in the proper form, and check your output for plausibility.

You may also wish to draw on other professional aids

during your study. Learn what permissions related to experimental subjects and to quoted material will be required for your work. Consult guides on ethical behavior to make sure you act responsibly toward your human or animal subjects.

Investigate relevant organizations and public servants as possible sources of data or other help for your project. If you are a foreign student doing research related to your home country, you may also wish to investigate area collections that have information on your country.

Consultants are another form of useful help. They may include statistical consultants, computer consultants, editors, content specialists, translators, and typists. Make sure that you and any consultant you hire have a clear understanding about the consultant's fees and responsibilities, and make sure that your committee approves your use of the consultant. Do not expect any consultant to take over the work that you yourself should perform.

After you have completed the research involved in your study, you will begin to prepare the dissertation that describes that research. The next chapter gives you specific guidance for preparing each chapter and section of your dissertation.

 NINE

Organizing and Writing the Dissertation

Kimberly's research study compared two methods of teaching English as a second language (ESL) to adult Spanish-speaking males. After preparing the front and back matter for her dissertation, she began to revise her proposal chapters so that they could become the first three chapters of the dissertation. In addition to more minor modifications, she explained in detail a change she had made in one of the methods of teaching that she tested; the change related to new instructional materials that she had found out about after she began her study, so it had not been included in her proposal.

The data from Kimberly's study included pretests and posttests of her subjects' ability to read and speak English and also responses to a questionnaire asking about their personal satisfaction with the teaching. She performed descriptive analyses including calculating the means and standard deviations for each of her variables and the correlations between the variables. She checked the plausibility of critical assumptions, such as the assumption that her frequency distributions were approximately normal in shape and the assumption that the pretest used as a covariate was independent of the methods. She then conducted the analyses she had planned in her proposal, including an analysis of covariance on the posttest data using the pretest as a covariate, and added a supplementary analysis of factors relating to the new instructional materials. Using a combination of statistics packages and graphics software available in her university computer center, she constructed tables and figures that showed the results of her analyses. These she placed, with accompanying text, in her results chapter.

In her summary and conclusions chapter, Kimberly summarized her results and drew conclusions about factors that seemed to hinder or facilitate the teaching of English as a second language to adults (as compared to techniques used with children, which she had discussed as part of the theoretical framework in her review of literature chapter). She compared the effectiveness of the teaching methods, as measured on tests, with the subjects' personal reactions to the teaching. She discussed the implications of her results for adult ESL teaching and recommended further research, including additional modifications and tests of one of the teaching methods.

Your dissertation is a written account of the completed study in which you demonstrate your ability to conduct research. It is the culmination of your doctoral program and the document you must defend at your final orals. Others will judge your ability as a researcher by it. For these reasons, you should make every effort to write a logical, coherent, accurate, and scholarly dissertation.

This chapter will explain how to organize and write your dissertation. The first section of the chapter describes the major parts of the dissertation and the content and structure of each part. The next section shows you how to develop the first three chapters of the dissertation, using the chapters of your proposal as bases. The third section presents guidelines for analysis of your data. The final two sections cover the last two chapters of the dissertation.

Structuring Your Dissertation

A dissertation usually has a standard format. Your graduate school undoubtedly publishes a format that you will be expected to follow. Most dissertations include the following parts:

Front matter
   Title page
   Approval page
   Abstract
   Acknowledgments
   Table of contents
   List of tables
   List of figures
Main body
   Introduction to the problem
   Review of literature
   Method
   Results
   Summary and conclusions
Back matter
   Bibliography or references
   Appendix(es)

Front Matter. The first page of the dissertation is the title page. The format of this page varies from one institution to another, but it usually includes the following items:

- the title of the study;
- the name of its author;
- the name of the program, department, or school;
- the name of the institution to which the dissertation is submitted;
- the degree for which the dissertation was prepared; and
- the year when the degree is conferred (or sometimes the date of presentation of the dissertation instead).

Exhibit 3 shows an example of a title page.

     Choose the title of your dissertation carefully. A good title is concise yet clearly indicates the nature and scope of the study. Key words and phrases in the title should be useful both

Exhibit 3. Example of a Title Page.

THE EFFECT OF MODIFYING A LOCUS OF CONTROL AND A
SELF-CONCEPT INSTRUMENT ON THE PREDICTION OF
ACHIEVEMENT OF DEAF ADOLESCENTS

by
William Harold Koelle

A Dissertation submitted to the School of Education
of
The Catholic University of America
in partial fulfillment of the requirements
for the degree of Doctor of Philosophy

May, 1981

---

to those who catalog your study and to researchers who scan a
bibliography or index in which your dissertation may be listed.
"Self-Concept, Locus of Control, and Achievement of a Handicapped Population" would be an inadequate title for our example dissertation because it is too vague about the relationships
involved. A better, but still inadequate, title might be, "Prediction of the Achievement of Deaf Adolescents on the Basis of
Self-Concept and Locus of Control Measures."

The approval page usually contains the names of the
members of your committee, with a place for each member to
sign after the defense of your dissertation is completed and all
necessary changes have been made. Not all institutions require
an approval page to be placed in the dissertation, however.

Some institutions require that an abstract be included in
the dissertation. This abstract can be the same one that is later
published in *Dissertation Abstracts International.* The abstract
is a brief summary of the purpose and content of the disserta-

tion. It follows the same structure as the dissertation, with emphasis on the statement of the problem, the methods, the results, and the conclusion. It should be fully comprehensible by someone who has not read the dissertation. Most potential readers of your dissertation will read the abstract first, so a clearly written, informative, and interesting abstract can greatly increase the readership of your study.

A page of acknowledgments is included in the dissertation so that you can name and thank people who have helped you in your study. Acknowledgments should be simple and restrained; effusive praise for routine help is unnecessary and in poor taste.

The table of contents provides an outline of the major parts of your dissertation. It begins with a list of the front matter, except for the title page and the table of contents page itself, with page references for each entry in lower-case Roman numerals. The chapters of the main body of the dissertation are listed next, with page references in Arabic numerals. Usually appropriate subheadings for each chapter are also included in the table of contents. For example, subheadings for the first chapter might be Context, Statement of the Problem, Hypotheses and Research Questions, Significance of the Study, Definition of Terms, and Assumptions and Limitations of the Study. Finally, the table of contents lists the back matter, with page references in Arabic numerals continuing serially from the main body of the dissertation.

Following the table of contents are separate pages for the List of Tables and the List of Figures. The full titles of tables and figures, worded exactly as they appear in the dissertation, should be presented along with their corresponding numbers (usually Arabic) and page references. Consult the guidelines provided by your university or your style manual for additional information regarding the pages in the front matter.

Main Body of the Dissertation. As previously mentioned, the dissertation normally is divided into five chapters, and our following discussion presupposes a five-chapter format. However, some dissertations contain four chapters because the review of literature is brief enough to be included in the first chapter. More than five chapters may be required in dissertations that involve historical research, extensive case studies, ethnographic research, or model building.

The first three chapters of a five-chapter dissertation are essentially the same as the proposal chapters described in our Chapters Five and Six. These chapters concern the introduction to the problem and the study, the review of the literature, and the design and methodology of the study, respectively. Your proposal chapters do not automatically become the first three chapters of your dissertation, however; they must be rewritten to reflect what actually occurred in your study before they will be acceptable.

The fourth chapter of the dissertation presents the results of your study. Occasionally the discussion of the results accompanies their presentation, but the discussion is most often reserved for the final chapter of the dissertation. The final chapter consists of a summary of the study, a discussion of the study (if this is not included in the fourth chapter), the study's conclusions, the implications for practice, and recommendations for further research. The organization and content of the last two chapters of the dissertation are discussed in detail later in this chapter.

Back Matter. The bibliography provides a complete description of the sources cited in your dissertation. Some style manuals distinguish between a bibliography and references. "References" is a listing only of those sources cited in the dissertation, while a bibliography contains all sources cited in the study plus those consulted by the researcher and, sometimes, a list of other selected sources. Some bibliographies have separate sections for books, periodicals, reports, and interviews, but most are arranged in a single alphabetized list. The style manual recommended or required by your university will specify the format of your bibliography and its entries.

An appendix, if included, follows the bibliography or references. The appendix contains any supporting materials that are not essential to the narrative in the main body of the dissertation. Such materials may include raw data, if feasible; complicated figures or tables; tables providing supplementary information; samples of detailed instructions, form letters, and permission slips; original instruments or instruments that are not easily accessible; long quotations; detailed statistical formulas; and results of a pilot study. Check your style manual for information concerning the format of the appendix.

Updating Your Proposal

Because the first three chapters of your dissertation will likely have the same structure and essentially the same content as the three chapters of a detailed proposal, you can use your proposal as a basis for writing these chapters. Modifications of the proposal are necessary, however, since the dissertation is an account of a *completed* study, while the proposal was an account of a *planned* study. The modifications, which usually are minor, will probably involve changing tense, updating and adding information, and describing how the study actually progressed rather than how it was planned to progress. If your department required only a brief proposal or no proposal at all, consult Chapters Five and Six of this text for further information concerning the structure and content of these three chapters.

The Introductory Chapter. The first chapter of your proposal should require only slight changes to become the first chapter of your dissertation. Change the tense throughout from future to past or present, as appropriate. Review each section of the chapter in light of the completed study and rewrite any sections that are not complete, accurate, or clearly written, or for which you now have better insight than you did when you wrote the proposal.

In particular, evaluate the adequacy of the theoretical framework you presented in the section on the context of the problem. Restructure this if necessary. Delete or add subproblem descriptions if changes were made as your study progressed. Restate any hypotheses that were not clearly written in the proposal. Review the rationale for each hypothesis and include its expected resolution based on the theoretical framework of your study. Define any important terms whose definitions were omitted in the proposal. If necessary, restate the arguments for the theoretical and practical significance of the study. Finally, add any limitations that may have been realized as a result of doing the study. After all modifications have been made, read the chapter several times. Carefully evaluate its suitability as the introduction to your study.

The Review of Literature Chapter. The review of literature from your proposal may require the addition of new or previously overlooked studies. After adding these studies, read the chapter carefully to determine whether it satisfies the criteria of a good review of literature given in Chapter Five. Is your review structured logically? Do its dimensions adequately reflect the focus of your study? Does the review have sufficient scope? Have you carefully selected the studies and the amount and kind of information included from each one? Have you used appropriate headings to guide the reader through the review? Have you integrated the review rather than simply produced an annotated bibliography? Finally, does the summary of the review provide a solid foundation for the theoretical framework and hypotheses of your study?

The Method Chapter. This chapter of the proposal will need the most extensive revisions in order to be appropriate for the dissertation. It must be changed to report what actually occurred in your study. As in the first chapter, changes in tense from future to past or present will be necessary. The sections on instruments, treatments, tasks, and materials should require little or no change, but review them for clarity, accuracy, and completeness. The remaining sections of this proposal chapter may need substantial modifications.

In the section on population and sample, describe your sampling procedures and tell how many individuals were selected for the sample. Describe the sample completely, providing information on all relevant characteristics such as sex, age, race, socioeconomic status, and IQ. Use tables and figures as necessary to display the characteristics of your sample. Provide enough information about your sample to let others judge its representativeness. If your sample consists of volunteers, describe how that sample might differ from a nonvolunteer sample or a random sample from the population. Report the occurrence of any dropouts from the sample and the reasons for dropping out, if they are known.

The procedures section should state exactly how the

study was conducted. List events in time sequence and tell who was involved in each. Describe completely what happened, when, and where. Indicate what the subjects were told and how they reacted. Include the findings of any pilot study you conducted and any procedural modifications that were made as a result of the pilot study. Finally, describe how the subjects were debriefed.

The section on design and data analysis should describe thoroughly the design of your study and the strategy you employed to analyze your data. Specify any models you used. Name or describe the statistical procedures used and the level of significance at which each hypothesis was tested. If you performed preliminary analyses to examine the plausibility of critical assumptions, report the results of these analyses here. Make this section of the chapter complete enough that no additional description of analyses will be necessary in your later chapter on results.

Analyzing Your Data

Analysis involves organizing, manipulating, and summarizing your data. Its purpose is to help you discover important patterns in your results. Analysis should reduce raw data to a form that allows the phenomena represented by those data to be described, examined, and interpreted.

Because of the wide variety of studies and kinds of data, it is not possible to present specific guidelines for your data analysis procedure. In general, we recommend that you follow these steps:

1. Conduct a series of descriptive analyses.
2. Check the plausibility of critical assumptions upon which your analyses depend.
3. Carry out the analyses you planned in your proposal.
4. Conduct supplementary analyses as needed.

Each of these steps is discussed further in the pages that follow.

Descriptive Analyses. Extensive descriptive analyses allow you to familiarize yourself thoroughly with your data as well as to provide summary data for your results chapter. First, obtain and carefully examine the frequency distribution of each variable, along with the appropriate indices of its central tendency (for example, mean, median, or mode) and its variability (for example, variance, standard deviation, or range). The shape, central tendency, and variability of the frequency distribution of a variable can provide clues about unusual occurrences related to the variable.

If a normal distribution is expected, check to see whether the frequency distribution is approximately normal in shape. A markedly skewed distribution for a test, for example, may indicate that the test was too hard (positive skewness) or too easy (negative skewness). A large amount of skewness in an attitude questionnaire indicates that the items in the instrument were not good discriminators. Variables with unusually small standard deviations may have a problem with restriction of range. An unexpectedly large standard deviation for a variable may indicate the presence of outliers, that is, individuals who do not properly belong in the population of interest. The central tendency and variability indices will enable you to compare the performance of subjects in your study with the performance of those in other studies that used the same variables and measures. Note any unexpected results and keep them in mind when you conduct analyses that address your hypotheses and research questions and when you discuss your results.

You should also obtain information about the relationship between the variables in your study. Calculate the correlations between pairs of variables or construct contingency tables or cross tabulations whenever at least one of the variables is measured on a nominal scale. If you use a Pearson product-moment correlation, examine the scatter plot for each relationship to determine whether it is linear. If it is nonlinear, a Pearson product-moment correlation will underestimate the strength of that relationship, and you will need to use a statistic that is appropriate for assessing the strength of a nonlinear relationship, such as the *eta* statistic (Nunnally, 1978).

Relationship information is important for examining the

suitability of a variable as a covariate in the analysis of covariance or detecting multicollinearity (moderate to high correlations among predictors) in regression analysis. If certain variables do not achieve an expected level of relationship, they should be examined for possible problems in the way they have been defined or for the presence of some artifact that has attenuated the index.

Third, obtain the mean and standard deviation for each group in the design as well as for aggregates of groups that are relevant to your hypotheses and research questions. For example, in a 3 (Reading Method) x 2 (Ability) design, you would obtain the mean and standard deviation for each of the six groups in the design as well as for each of the three Reading Method groups and each of the two Ability groups. This information, in addition to being needed for tables in your results chapter, will help you interpret the results of your analyses.

Assumptions. You should examine the likelihood that assumptions necessary for proper interpretation of the results of certain statistical procedures are true. These are the assumptions for which a particular statistical procedure is not robust; that is, it cannot be violated without serious consequences for the analysis. Chapter Six presented some examples of such assumptions. Usually you examine the plausibility of an assumption by performing some statistical analysis on the data. For example, for the assumption of homogeneity of regression (parallel within-group regression lines) in the analysis of covariance, you would test the null hypothesis of no difference between the population regression parameters. If this hypothesis is rejected, you would question the correctness of the assumption. On the other hand, if this hypothesis is not rejected, you would normally proceed as if the assumption were correct.

Often you can obtain the information needed to examine the plausibility of an assumption at the same time as you analyze the data using the statistical procedure that requires the assumption. This is especially true when you use computer programs for data analysis, since many programs include tests of critical assumptions. If you judge critical assumptions to be plausible, then proceed with the data analysis as scheduled. If a critical assumption appears to be violated, employ whatever alternative strategy you specified in your proposal.

Planned Analyses. Next, conduct the analyses that were outlined in the data analysis section of your proposal. If that section was carefully planned, you need only progress through your outline step by step, taking care of contingencies as they arise. You will likely use standard statistical procedures to analyze quantitative data. These procedures generally involve calculations of summary statistics and insertion of these into standard formulas, after which analysis proceeds in a relatively straightforward fashion. If the calculations are either extensive because of a large amount of data or complex because of the nature of the statistical procedures, you should probably use a computer to perform the analysis. Most major statistical computer packages include a full complement of procedures, both descriptive and inferential, parametric and nonparametric, and univariate and multivariate. The use of computers for data analysis was described in Chapter Eight.

Qualitative data include interview data, documents, photographs, artifacts, and field notes. If your data are qualitative, you will need to provide a structure to help you understand the information contained in the data and report it in your dissertation. The process of analyzing qualitative data is an art as well as a science (Guba and Lincoln, 1981).

Ordinarily, structure is provided to qualitative data through the use of preordained categories that allow the data to be coded and classified. Bogdan and Biklen (1982) provide several coding categories by which qualitative data may be structured. The structure chosen will both limit and be limited by the researcher. It provides a focus for the data analysis that determines to a great extent what the researcher will be able to learn from the data, but at the same time, the structure depends on the insights of the researcher concerning the data and on the choice of appropriate categories. Excellent presentations of ways to organize and analyze qualitative data are given by Bogdan and Biklen (1982), Schatzman and Strauss (1973), and Spradley (1979, 1980).

Supplementary Analyses. Further analyses of the data often are performed following the completion of the planned analyses. These additional analyses may be made necessary by oversights in the proposal concerning the data analysis, occurrence of unanticipated outcomes, or additional questions that result from your increased awareness of the problem as you become involved in the data analysis.

When you worked out the data analysis plan described in your proposal, you may have overlooked useful analytic procedures. This often happens if the design is complex or contains multiple independent or dependent variables. For example, as your data analysis proceeds, you may realize the need to produce some combinations of the independent variables, the dependent variables, or both in order to address more appropriately some of your research questions or hypotheses. Also, if your planned analyses had contingencies, you may not have considered all possible alternative strategies when you wrote the proposal. Other alternate analyses may become apparent as you analyze the data.

Unanticipated outcomes can result either from failure to support some hypotheses or from the presence of unusual data such as extreme skewness, many apparent outliers, very limited variability, or unexpectedly low correlations. When the data do not support hypotheses, you are obliged to examine plausible reasons, and these examinations may require additional analyses. Subsequent analyses may also be required to determine the cause of unusual occurrences or to proceed with the analysis of the research questions and hypotheses in the light of these occurrences.

Finally, as a result of your increased insights into the problem as the study proceeds, you may generate additional research questions that you decide to address, either for completeness or for the support of speculations that you intend to make when discussing your results. The analyses you planned earlier may not be appropriate for these additional questions, so you will need to add new ones.

Results Chapter

The fourth chapter of your dissertation contains a complete account of the results of your data analysis. After you have performed all the analyses and are satisfied with your interpretation of the outcomes, you should present the results clearly and succinctly. Use narrative form, accompanied by tables and figures. Present the results in sufficient detail to enable other researchers to reanalyze your data. If you do not provide the raw data in an appendix to your dissertation, you should indicate where they can be obtained.

Generally, the results chapter presents the following:

- summary descriptive data for the entire sample, for individual groups, and for other reasonable aggregates;
- results of the planned statistical analyses that address the hypotheses and research questions;
- results of important subsequent analyses; and
- decisions concerning each null hypothesis and the apparent resolution of each research question.

Use tables frequently throughout the chapter, and include supporting figures as needed.

Organization. You should decide on the organization of your results chapter before you start to write it. Three possible organizers for this chapter are hypotheses, variables, and time. Tuckman (1972) recommends using hypotheses to organize the presentation of results. The hypotheses become subheadings for the parts of the chapter. Each subheading should be followed by these items:

- a brief restatement of the hypothesis;
- the data related to that hypothesis, with accompanying tables and figures;
- the statistical decision concerning the null hypothesis, along with evidence from the appropriate statistical procedures; and
- an assessment of whether the data support or fail to support the research hypothesis.

Sometimes it is more convenient to present the data by variable (for example, self-concept, age, sex, achievement subtests) or in a time sequence (pretest results, posttest results, retention test results). Decide on the organization that best fits the nature of your study and your data. If the organization of your chapter is not by hypotheses, you should provide a summary of findings at the end of the chapter in which you discuss each hypothesis and summarize the evidence for its support or nonsupport.

Before writing the text for your results chapter, construct all the tables and figures you intend to include in it. The chapter organization and the sequence of tables will mutually influence each other. You may find that you change the organization of your chapter as you attempt to construct comprehensive and mutually exclusive tables. Once you are satisfied with the sequence of tables, use the tables as a guide to writing the text.

If you have conducted a qualitative research study, the organization of your results chapter may differ from that used for a quantitative study. Just as you would do if you had hypotheses, you will want to establish a perspective on an issue and then present evidence concerning it from your data. The evidence may take the form of direct quotations from participants, a detailed case narrative, a summary of interview data, an analysis of the context of a situation, or an analysis of documents. If you have appropriate data, you should also include evidence from a quantitative perspective, using tables where appropriate.

Bogdan and Biklen (1982) summarize the task of presenting results from a qualitative research study as follows: "A good qualitative paper is well-documented with description taken from the data to illustrate and substantiate the assertions made. There are no formal conventions used to establish truth in a qualitative research paper. Your task is to convince the reader of the plausibility of your presentation" (p. 177).

Tables. In most situations, tables are essential for the presentation of descriptive data and the results of statistical analyses. Use tables freely in your dissertation, but remember that the intent of a table is to supplement, not to duplicate, the text. Your text should refer to each table and discuss its highlights; but if every entry in the table is mentioned in the text, the table becomes unnecessary. Prepare text and tables so that each can stand apart from the other. A reader should be able to understand the text without consulting the tables, and each table should also be self-explanatory. Make your tables intelligible by using descriptive titles, careful format, subheadings, and notes or footnotes for clarification. Consult your style manual for guidelines concerning the construction, format, and title of tables.

Tables make it easier for you to present your data and for others to understand and compare them. Before deciding what format is best for a table or even whether you need a table at all, determine the amount and complexity of the data you wish to present. If the amount is large or the data are complex, use of a table can help you avoid a cumbersome or confusing narrative that may obscure important relationships. For example, you can easily present a series of correlations in a table containing a correlation matrix, or you can present the results of an analysis of variance in a summary table, but presenting such sets of data only in text would be laborious at best. However, not all statistical data need to be placed in tables. A simple statement such as the following would be inserted directly into the text: "Of the ninety-two deaf adolescents in the study, eighty had normal-hearing parents, nine had two hearing-impaired parents, and three had one hearing-impaired parent and one normal-hearing parent."

The nature of your study will dictate the number and kind of tables you need to include in your dissertation. Generally, tables should cover both relevant descriptive data and the results of statistical analyses. Examples of descriptive data that fit well in tables include mean and standard deviation of each variable for the entire sample, along with the size of the sample; correlations or cross-tabulations between variables; mean and standard deviation for each variable in each group of the design, along with the size of the group; and mean and standard deviation of each aggregated variable corresponding to the questions and hypotheses being addressed in the study (for example, means and standard deviations of the main effects or of the interactions in an analysis of variance).

You should also use tables to summarize results of statistical analyses, such as the analysis of variance, the analysis of covariance, and regression analysis. Sometimes a single table will combine both descriptive data and the results of a statistical analysis. For example, the results of a *t* test normally are included in a table with the mean, standard deviation, size of each group, and the observed value of the *t* statistic. Place tables containing nonessential data or very complex tables in the appendix.

The results of any planned comparisons between group means are usually reported in a table. However, for *post hoc* procedures you usually should report only the decisions resulting from these tests, not the specific calculations involved. If you do report the calculations, they should be placed in the appendix.

Figures. Figures include graphs, charts, diagrams, maps, photographs, and drawings. When used properly, figures can highlight the presentation of the results of your dissertation. They are particularly useful to demonstrate data, ideas, or relationships that are more easily presented and comprehended in a visual than in a written medium.

Figures should not substitute for textual descriptions, but rather should emphasize particular aspects of the results. A figure does not provide verification for a finding; only statistical or other evidence can do that. The figure's job is to help in the interpretation of the finding by illustrating it. For example, in a graph representing a possible interaction between two variables in an analysis of variance design, the presence of nonparallel lines is not sufficient evidence for the presence of an interaction. However, if the statistical analysis reveals a significant interaction, the graph can be a valuable aid for understanding that interaction.

Figures should be used sparingly, but do not hesitate to use a figure when you think it is needed. Some examples of situations in which a figure would be helpful are the following:

• trends in data collection over time;
• interactions in the analysis of variance and regression analysis;
• scatter plots in correlational analysis;

- plots of residuals in regression analysis;
- plots of discriminant functions, principal components, clusters, and factors in various multivariate analyses; and
- results of structural paths or models.

Many of the qualities of good tables also apply to figures. Perhaps the most important quality is that the figure be simple enough to communicate the intended idea. Complex figures may obscure patterns rather than highlight them. Consult your style manual for information concerning the proper format for figures.

Summary and Conclusions Chapter

The fifth chapter of your dissertation ordinarily contains the following:

- a summary of your study;
- discussion of your findings in light of the study's theoretical framework;
- specific conclusions you are able to make;
- implications of the results for practice; and
- recommendations for further research.

Some dissertations discuss findings when they are presented in the results chapter, but most students find it easier to discuss their findings after all of their results have been presented so they can make use of all the findings in the discussion.

Summary. The final chapter of the dissertation usually begins with a summary of the context of the study, its methodology, and its major findings. This summary provides the reader with an overview of what has already been presented and an orientation to the remainder of the chapter. Often people interested in your study will read this chapter first, so a clearly written, inclusive summary is important for the proper understanding of the rest of the chapter. The summary should be brief, however; usually two or three pages will suffice. In the summary, restate the problem and the purpose of your study and review its theoretical framework, major questions and hypotheses, procedures, and data analysis. Then present the major findings of the study in terms of the statistical decisions made concerning the hypotheses or the apparent answers to the research questions. The discussion of the findings ordinarily follows this summary.

Discussion. If the review of literature is the heart of the proposal, then the discussion section is the soul of the dissertation. The review of literature chapter presented the theoretical framework underlying the study; the discussion section presents your interpretation of your findings in light of that theoretical framework. This section, more than any other, emphasizes the *you* in your study. As the researcher, you have been closer to the study, its foundations, its progress, and its data than any other individual. You now have the opportunity, indeed the responsibility, to tell others what your findings mean, how they fit into your theoretical framework, and what you have concluded about the hypotheses and research questions that you raised earlier. Of course, all that you say must be accompanied by supporting evidence. Writing this section demands full knowledge of your data and its theoretical framework as well as considerable insight, creativity, and perseverance.

Van Dalen (1979) has characterized the interpretation and discussion of results as one of the most delightful and difficult phases of the dissertation. Many who have completed a dissertation will attest to the difficulty of this phase, but not many to its delightfulness—at least not if you ask them while they are still immersed in the process. However, there is no reason why this phase cannot be an enjoyable one for you. Since there is no required format for this section, the following guidelines may help you structure the section so that its writing can proceed smoothly.

The major issues raised in the first chapter of the dissertation should be addressed in this section, so organize your discussion around examination of these issues. Hypotheses, research questions, and variables can all be used to provide structure. Some directors prefer certain structures, usually those provided by hypotheses, so you should confer with your director concerning his or her preferences. You need not follow the same organization in this chapter as you did in the previous chapter, since the best organization for presentation of results is not necessarily the best one for interpretation of these results.

Within each subsection of your discussion section, proceed from the particular to the general. You will recall that the review of literature chapter went from the general to the particular, dealing first with the overall context of the problem and relevant theories and then going on to specific studies and issues of immediate concern to the study. Reverse this structure in the discussion section.

First, discuss each issue in light of the findings of your study. State the issue and present the findings that relate to it. Designate relevant hypotheses as supported or unsupported and specific findings as expected or unexpected, giving reasons for each designation. Make tentative interpretations as to what the apparent facts are and what functional relationships seem to exist. Finally, identify uncontrolled variables that may have affected the results and discuss their possible implications.

Second, indicate what relationships exist between your findings and those of other researchers. Compare your findings with the findings of other studies from your theoretical framework, both those that were supported by your results and those that were not. Discuss particular reasons why your findings differ from those in the latter group. Then evaluate the legitimacy of the interpretation of your findings compared to the larger body of empirical work.

Third, discuss the theoretical implications of your findings based on an evaluation of all available evidence. This discussion takes into account your findings, the findings of others, relevant theories, the assumptions you have made, and recognized limitations of your study.

The discussion of a particular issue is fairly straightforward when your results support the hypotheses related to that issue. Since hypotheses have been formulated on the basis of theory or previous empirical research, confirmation of these hypotheses enables you to develop arguments for the relationship of your findings to the earlier work. When your results and your hypotheses agree, you can devote most of your discussion section to the theoretical implications of your findings.

If your results do not support your hypotheses, the discussion becomes more difficult to write. In addition to discussing the major issues raised in the introductory chapter, you need to identify and discuss plausible reasons why this lack of support occurred. These reasons normally involve the hypotheses themselves and/or the assumptions, design, and procedures of your study.

When searching for plausible reasons for results that failed to support your hypotheses, start with a reexamination of the theory and related studies that constituted your theoretical framework. The theory may not be well established, or the previous research may be quite tentative or based on very few studies. They may therefore have led to inaccurate predictions, and your results are merely detecting this inaccuracy. If the theory is well established and the evidence from previous research is convincing, however, it is unlikely that failure to support your hypotheses was the result of a faulty theoretical framework. In that case you should seriously question the theory or previous research only after systematically eliminating all other possibilities.

It may be that your hypotheses were based on inappropriate interpretation of the theory and previous research. If your reasoning is flawed, the problem is not with the theoretical framework but with your hypotheses. You should discuss that possibility in this section.

Next, you should consider failure to satisfy your assumptions as a possible cause of failing to support your hypotheses. Some of the assumptions underlying your study may not have been correct. For example, suppose you do not control for socioeconomic status because you assume that it will not influence the variables in your study. If your assumption is false, then the failure to include socioeconomic status in your design may increase the error in your analysis to a degree that prevents you from obtaining statistically significant results for some of the factors in your design. It may be possible to examine the plausibility of some assumptions by using the data from your study, but other assumptions may prove difficult to examine and must be presumed. You should discuss the potential effects of failing to meet some assumptions and indicate the likelihood that these assumptions were not met in your study.

Next, examine your research design for potential problems. You may have failed to adequately control for one or more threats to internal validity, anticipate certain happenings that affected the outcome of your study, or make appropriate decisions concerning some aspect of the design. Some aspects of the research design in which problems may have occurred are presented in the following pages. You should discuss any of these aspects that may have been a factor in your study.

First, the predictions specified by the hypotheses may not be true for the particular population chosen for your study. Past research that has supported the hypotheses may not have used this population. Your assumption that the hypothesized results would also apply to this population may not have been correct.

Second, a problem may have occurred with sampling. Assuming the population selected was appropriate, the sample may not have been representative of that population because of improper sampling procedures, a large amount of nonresponse, or the use of a special sample such as volunteers. Lack of representativeness could bias the results of your study by failing to control for certain variables that were related to the dependent variable in the sampled group in a manner different from the nonsampled group.

Third, proper control of important variables or conditions may have been lacking. Perhaps the design either did not consider some important variable or did not anticipate certain happenings that affected the dependent variable. Control is compromised when random assignment to groups is not possible or when threats to internal validity are overlooked. You should explore the likelihood of such threats occurring and discuss them when necessary.

Fourth, the treatment may have been flawed or may not have operated as expected. Perhaps the treatment itself was not a proper reflection of the theory or previous research. Your assumptions that the treatment would have the same effect on all participants or would produce effective results may have been incorrect.

Fifth, there may have been problems with the instruments used in the study. Perhaps the traits of interest were not properly measured because the instruments lacked adequate construct validity. The instruments may have been too easy or too hard, resulting in ceiling and floor effects, respectively. You should review the appropriateness of each instrument, especially if you used scores from any of them as a dependent variable.

The one aspect of the research design that should not be a reason for failing to obtain support for hypotheses is the data analysis strategy. Once data are available, you can keep trying analyses until you find a satisfactory one. If a planned data analysis proves inappropriate or inadequate, perform other analyses. Exclusion of certain sources of data and insufficient sample size can influence data analyses and render a particular analysis insensitive to certain effects. However, both specification of variables and determination of sample size occur prior to analysis in the design stage of the study. Thus poor design can be a possible reason for not supporting a hypothesis, but improper data analysis should never be.

How should you treat a situation in which your results are not statistically significant, but the data show an obvious trend that supports your research hypotheses? Some researchers might advise ignoring the trend, while others would insist upon incorporating the trend information into the discussion, with proper qualification. This controversial issue rests on the nature of the hypothesis testing model, a decision model with a probabilistic framework. The decision categories are determined by the choice of the level of significance made prior to obtaining the data. If the statistical procedure used to test the null hypothesis fails to produce a significant value, then the null hypothesis is not rejected. Technically, this failure to reject means that you do not have any evidence for the difference between the population parameters being estimated. Your discussion of the research hypothesis should proceed as if you had failed to support it. However, many researchers recognize trends toward significance if the result from the statistical procedure they are using occurs at a probability level between .05 and .20.

When the data show an obvious trend (a probability for an observed value less than .10 or even .20 in some cases) but statistically significant differences are not present, you should proceed in your discussion section as follows:

1. State clearly your statistical decision, based on the level of significance that you have chosen and the appropriate research decision regarding the hypothesis.
2. Indicate the consequences of failing to support the hypothesis.
3. Indicate what trend you see in the data; describe what the trend suggests and to what extent the trend supports your hypothesis.
4. Evaluate the failure to find statistically significant differences. If statistical artifacts such as low power or extremely high variability are present, you might argue more strongly for the support of your hypothesis, especially if the support from the theoretical framework is strong. If the differences are small and the amount of variability is reasonable, it is not likely that any true differences exist, and your discussion should acknowledge this.

When discussing results and suggesting explanations, choose your words carefully. Use qualifiers such as *seems, appears, possible, probably, likely,* or *unlikely* when attributing causality to some variable, suggesting alternative explanations, generalizing to the population, or suggesting reasons why certain events occurred as they did in your study.

The verb *prove* should be avoided when referring to hypotheses. You do not *prove* hypotheses; you confirm them, support them, or fail to confirm them. (The one thing you do prove in doing your study is your ability to complete it!) The hypothesis testing model is based on a probabilistic framework. The probability of rejecting or confirming a hypothesis is never equal to unity, since there is always the possibility, however small, that you have rejected a true null hypothesis falsely (committed a Type I error) or failed to reject a false null hypothesis (committed a Type II error). The word *prove* is reserved for disciplines such as mathematics and philosophy that use axiomatic rather than probabilistic methods to arrive at conclusions.

Similarly, you do not *disprove* any hypothesis or theory when you fail to reject a null hypothesis. This failure to reject means simply that you do not have enough evidence to dispute the null hypothesis; it does not mean that you should act as if the null hypothesis is true and then proceed to argue the implications of that truth for your theoretical framework.

Conclusions. This section should state those facts about your study that you are willing to call conclusions. Conclusions are very important, since they involve your evaluation of your findings in light of your theoretical framework. A one-to-one correspondence does not necessarily exist between findings and conclusions. Generally, findings support conclusions.

You will have to defend your conclusions more than any other statements in your dissertation, so do not state them casually. In structuring this section, relate your conclusions to the major issues they address. Based on your findings, what can you now say about each of these issues? How convincing is your evidence? You might also include in this section statements about noteworthy incidental findings that were not concerned directly with the major issues of your study. It is helpful to include a brief commentary for each conclusion rather than simply listing a series of propositions.

Some directors prefer that conclusions be incorporated into the discussion section along with the discussion; however, the importance of conclusions certainly seems to warrant their inclusion in a separate section.

Implications for Practice. Your findings are likely to have some practical implications, particularly if you performed applied research, from which practical applications usually flow directly. Applications may follow even from studies that are classified as basic research.

Discussion of the practical implications of your study is

very important, since every behavioral science discipline has an applied aspect. For example, dissertations in education might include a section on applications for teachers, instructional designers, administrators, or counselors. Dissertations in psychology might include a section on applications for clinicians, trainers, mental health professionals, or families. Dissertations in nursing might include a section on applications for nursing specialties, nurse practitioners, administrators, or nutritionists. Your ability to suggest applications is a mark of your understanding of the way your study relates to your profession.

Recommendations for Further Research. This section contains recommendations for ways that your study can be improved or the body of research to which it contributes can be extended further. These recommendations arise from constraints imposed on your study, the removal of which might produce different results; your recognition of variables or conditions that you were unable to control or were not interested in controlling; and your insights concerning direct extensions of your work, such as use of different populations or related questions, or further confirmation of your findings.

You are obliged to suggest possible ways in which your study can be improved or extended. After all, you are more informed about your study than anyone else. You have immersed yourself in its data, pondered its intricacies, and evaluated each of its aspects. You have reflected on the study's findings and their interpretation. In short, you are the best person to suggest extensions to your study. These suggestions can be very helpful to other researchers, especially other graduate students.

Summary

Your dissertation is the culmination of your graduate degree program and the product by which, more than anything else, your fitness to enter the scholarly community will be judged. It also represents a good deal of your time and effort. You will therefore want to write it as carefully as possible.

Most dissertations contain five main chapters: Introduction to the Problem, Review of Literature, Method, Results, and Summary and Conclusions. They also contain front and back matter. This chapter described the contents of all these parts of the dissertation in detail and gave directions for preparing them.

The first section of the chapter described the structure of the dissertation. It also explained the nature of the front and back matter, including the title page, the approval page, the abstract, the acknowledgments page, the table of contents, the lists of tables and figures, the bibliography or references, and the appendix.

The first three chapters of your dissertation are likely to be updated versions of the three chapters of your proposal. The second section of this chapter gave tips on how to update each proposal chapter for use in your dissertation.

Now that you have collected your data, you must analyze it before you can present it in your dissertation. Our chapter's third section suggested steps in that analysis, including descriptive analyses, examination of assumptions, planned analyses, and supplementary analyses.

The fourth chapter of your disertation contains a complete account of the results of your data analysis. Our chapter's fourth section suggested ways to organize your Results chapter and to use tables and figures in it.

Your dissertation's final chapter is the Summary and Conclusions chapter. It contains a summary of your study, discussion of your findings, specific conclusions that you drew, implications of your results for practice, and recommendations for further research. Our chapter gave advice on preparation of all these sections, with special tips for handling the discussion section in cases where your study's findings did not support your hypotheses.

The last step in the pursuit of your advanced degree is your final oral defense. The next chapter describes what usually happens in an oral defense and gives you advice on how to prepare for it.

 TEN

Ensuring
a Successful Defense

Vincent hoped to combine his vocation for the priesthood with a career in social work. His dissertation, a case study of a halfway house for teenage drug addicts that was run by his church, was based on long hours of participant observation. Vincent was the first to admit that he was very emotionally involved with his work and excited about the success that the halfway house seemed to be achieving.

His director and committee respected Vincent's enthusiasm, but they used his final oral defense to test his ability to blend it with objectivity. His director asked questions that forced him to compare his church's rehabilitation program with similar ones run by other churches and by secular organizations. Another committee member questioned the thoroughness of Vincent's analysis of data on recidivism and wondered if his sample of subjects was large enough to justify some of the conclusions he had drawn in his dissertation. Vincent had expected this kind of questioning, however, so he was able to respond accurately and politely, without becoming defensive.

The chairwoman of the defense committee, a professor in the political science department, turned the discussion to sources of funding for programs like Vincent's, questioning in particular the role of government funds in drug rehabilitation programs. Another committee member questioned whether halfway house programs were effective at all. Vincent found himself discussing social and moral issues that went well beyond the scope of his original study, but his work at the halfway house had given him a lot of practice in thinking on his feet. He managed to turn a potentially hostile encounter into a pleasant, scholarly discussion. He was given an unconditional pass, and both he and his program received high praise.

If you had attended a medieval European university, you would have done much of your academic work unsupervised. When you thought you were ready, you would have presented yourself to a committee of examiners who would have tried to determine whether the months and years you spent in acquiring knowledge had profited you. These examiners would have made stringent tests of the breadth and depth of your learning before deciding whether to welcome you into the fraternity of scholars.

Many faculty members still maintain this perspective. To them, the fact that you have completed your course work, comprehensive examinations, and dissertation is not enough. They feel that you must be able to vigorously defend yourself, your knowledge, your dissertation, and your program at a comprehensive final oral examination before you deserve to be called a scholar. Other faculty members, however, see the completion of your written dissertation as the culminating experience of your graduate work. They regard the final oral as largely a social formality during which you are officially welcomed into the scholarly fraternity.

Purposes of the Defense

In our view, the final oral defense of a dissertation has the following purposes:

- to serve as the final check on the adequacy of your dissertation and to make you show your ability to support and justify all parts of your study;

- to verify that you personally completed each aspect of your study;
- to establish that you can not only collect information and accurately report it but also intelligently evaluate it and draw logical conclusions, further hypotheses, and practical applications from it; and
- to check on the adequacy of the scope of your academic preparation as reflected in your ability to understand and respond to scholarly questions in the area in which you claim competence.

In verifying the adequacy of your dissertation, the examining committee's questions will relate to the substance of the dissertation itself. In checking to make sure you did the work you claim to have done, they will test your personal knowledge of all aspects of it. If you have in fact turned out a good product with which you are entirely familiar, you should have little trouble with questions in these areas.

In assessing your ability as a scholar rather than a technician, faculty members will expect you to show that you can think creatively and articulate intelligently under the stressful conditions of a final oral. They will ask you to suggest practical applications of your results and to integrate information and issues that you did not directly research with data that you did examine. They will try to discover whether you know more than what is printed in your dissertation abstract.

In determining the overall adequacy of your academic preparation, the examiners' questions may range far from the subject of your dissertation. Some institutions indeed prohibit examiners from asking questions about the methodology and adequacy of your study's research design and encourage them instead to make you demonstrate general competence in your field.

To learn your institution's views on the purposes of the final defense, read through the official literature it distributes, ask your director for his or her opinions, and ask students who have done their dissertations under your director what their experience in final orals was like.

Who May Be Present

The final oral is generally carried out in front of five or more individuals, including your dissertation committee and one or more examiners from outside your department. Generally one of the outside examiners serves as chairperson of the examining committee and another as recording secretary. If your institution has a policy of open orals, other faculty, even other students, may attend. In this case you might consider having a few friends come to your defense as your personal "cheering section."

Your director will usually want you to do well. After all, a sterling performance on your part also validates his or her good judgment and skill. The feelings of your other committee members will probably depend largely on the amount of time they have spent working with you. If they have been closely involved with you throughout the dissertation process, then they, too, are likely to be on your side at the time of your final oral. Since dissertation committee members usually outnumber outside examiners, you will most likely find that if your dissertation committee is satisfied with you and maintains its cohesion, the examining committee vote will be positive.

How to Prepare

In many ways, the final oral is like the proposal defense; therefore, most of the general advice given in Chapter Seven holds here, too. As with the proposal defense, consult with your director well ahead of time about the procedures of the final oral in your university. Make certain you know what your director expects. In fact, if your director is willing, ask what his or her first question or two might be so that you can prepare for them. This way, you will have a chance to respond intelligently in the examination while getting over your initial nervousness. If this procedure proves unacceptable, practice responding orally to questions about your project similar to ones you believe the examining committee is likely to ask.

You may want to have friends help you by setting up a mock final. You might also attend the final oral of another student, if possible. Observing "the real thing" usually makes the whole process less frightening.

Try to find out just where your oral will be held. Look over the room and, if you have the opportunity, practice presenting your summary statement there. Check the room for any equipment you might need, such as a blackboard, an overhead projector, or a screen. Make sure to arrange for these items well in advance of your defense if any proves to be missing. Check to make certain that all necessary paperwork has been correctly filed before your examination, too. Then read your dissertation through shortly before your defense. A dissertation is often put together in pieces, and a recent review of the complete document can help you see it once again as a whole.

It is a good idea to find out what has recently appeared in journals pertaining to your topic. Defense committee members sometimes ask a candidate questions based on recently published work just to see whether he or she has kept up with the field. Try to be especially aware if a member of your examining committee has recently published anything related to your subject.

Get a good night's sleep before your defense. There's no substitute for being thoroughly rested and well fed. Try not to have an extremely heavy meal just before your exam, however. You can celebrate afterward.

Dress the part. Even if every member of your examining committee comes to your final oral in blue jeans and a T-shirt, you should wear a suit or dress or other appropriate business attire. Let your clothes show your committee that you believe this final examination is important.

What Happens During the Defense

Oral defenses usually begin with the committee chairperson introducing the committee and explaining the procedures to be followed. You are then expected to introduce yourself, make a brief statement about your background, and present a fifteen- or twenty-minute summary of your study. This summary, which you have planned and practiced in advance, should cover all the major aspects of your research, but briefly. For example, mention the statistical analyses you used but do not go into a detailed exposition of statistical formulas. Should someone on the examining committee be interested in such detail, he or she may ask a question about it later.

Questions from the examiners follow your presentation. These questions and your answers will occupy most of the time in the oral defense. Questions may be asked in sequence, one examiner being allotted a certain amount of time and then passing to the next, or the committee may opt for a free-for-all method. Sometimes committees begin in an orderly fashion and end in a free-for-all. While some candidates hope for a free-for-all during which the examiners will spend most of the time talking with each other, it is usually better to begin with a more orderly round of questioning and let it gradually become a scholarly discussion among peers about the issues raised by your research. Such a sequence allows you to warm up on questions asked by people involved with you and thus builds your confidence about entering a professional discussion with your examiners. If you have a choice, opt for this slower-paced and more orderly format; at least suggest your preference to your director in advance of your defense.

Don't be afraid of questions, especially those that deal directly with your dissertation. You should have two powerful allies to help you deal with such questions—a committed director and the dissertation itself. Remember that you know more about your dissertation than anyone else in the room.

Make certain that you understand the particulars of each question being asked. If you launch into an answer to a question that you do not completely understand, you may expose more areas of concern than the questioner intended or confuse the questioner by responding to something he or she did not ask. As suggested in Chapter Seven, clarify your understanding by paraphrasing each question before responding to it. This also gives you a little extra time to formulate your reply. When you do answer, do so directly and succinctly. Do not keep talking just to fill up time.

Most examiners will want to know why you did your research; what you learned from your study; what practical and theoretical implications follow from your results; and what further research you think is needed on the same topic. They may also be interested in a candid evaluation of weaknesses you noted in your research design or procedures and limits to the meaningfulness of your study. Do not be overly harsh in criticizing your own work, however.

Many students have difficulty in discussing the extent to which their findings can be generalized and the practical implications that can be drawn from their results. It is better not to overgeneralize, since the findings from a single study usually cannot be applied with confidence. Still, you should not be afraid to describe the implications that you believe could be drawn from your results if they withstand the test of additional investigation.

Sometimes final oral defenses become dialogues among the examining committee members, almost to the exclusion of the candidate. Faculty members are not above trying to impress one another in an open forum. The committee chairperson should be able to keep such dialogues to a minimum, but, if not, be patient while you look for an opportunity to enter the discussion and draw it back to the topic at hand. Most of the committee members will likely be both grateful and impressed if you find a way to redirect the discussion in a professional manner.

You will know your oral is going well when your presentation and response to initial questions causes the examination to turn into a scholarly discussion in which you take a comfortable part. Then the examination becomes one of ideas, not of you, the candidate. This is more likely to happen if you are confident enough to disagree with your examiners on occasion and can support your opinions by evidence. Being able to stand your ground on a controversial issue is considered a sign of professional maturity.

No matter how well prepared you are for your final oral, you are bound to be somewhat nervous. This is perfectly normal, and any reasonable committee will expect it. Should you find yourself getting flustered, pause a moment to regain your composure.

The Final Decision

After the examining committee has completed its questioning, you and all visitors will be asked to leave the room. The committee then discusses your performance, usually including both your comportment during the oral examination and the quality of your dissertation. Finally, a vote is taken. The discussion and vote takes place behind closed doors both to allow the committee members to be more frank and to protect your privacy. It can also protect your dissertation committee against charges of excessive favoritism.

All members of the examining committee usually vote. In many institutions the vote must be a consensus of all present. In other institutions a two-thirds or three-quarters majority is needed. Candidates are rarely passed on a simple majority.

As with proposal defenses, decisions other than a simple pass or fail have become increasingly common. In the case of a conditional pass with minor revisions, your dissertation director will usually monitor these revisions. If major revisions are required, your dissertation may have to be approved by the entire examining committee, each signing off on it individually, or the committee may postpone a decision until a revised text is presented and a second oral is held.

A vote to fail a student is rare, but it can happen. If it should happen to you, ask the specific reasons for the committee's decision. Based upon these reasons, you can decide whether to launch an appeal or take some other action. Overturning rejection is no easy matter, however, and an attempt to do so should be undertaken only with the best advice and after a great deal of soul searching.

Once the examining committee has reached a consensus, you will usually be invited back into the examination room to hear the results. An unconditional pass means that from that moment you are, for all practical purposes, the holder of the degree you were pursuing. A conditional pass with minor revisions is generally considered a pass, the assumption being that the suggested revisions will be easily and quickly done. You should not delay in performing them, however, since you cannot presume that you hold the degree until they have been made.

A conditional pass with a request for major revisions means that the examining committee is dissatisfied with one or more important aspects of your dissertation. If you receive this vote, try to learn exactly what was found wanting. Knowing the specific requirements will help you determine how long it will take to make them and whether it is worth the effort. You should also make sure that you know the procedures for gaining full approval, including whether the committee is recommending or requiring another oral defense. Although hearing that you must make major revisions is bound to take the wind out of your sails, now is not the time to abandon ship. Save the crying, if any, for later and muster your resources to ask the right questions while the committee's ideas are still fresh. Remember that a conditional pass, even with extensive revisions required, is still a positive vote.

Sometimes an examining committee finds fault only with a student's oral presentation, perhaps because the student had an anxiety attack so severe that he or she could not continue an oral defense. In such cases the student will usually be required to schedule another defense but will not be otherwise penalized.

Afterward

Every institution has its own requirements concerning the format and disposition of a completed, approved dissertation. If your graduate school participates in the publishing program of University Microfilms International (UMI), you will be required to supply an abstract of 350 words or less along with your dissertation for reproduction on microfilm. Your abstract will be printed and published in *Dissertation Abstracts International* and will be indexed in the *Comprehensive Dissertation Index*.

UMI can act as your agent in applying for copyright of the dissertation, including preparation of the application and

submission of the required deposit copies and fees to the United
States Copyright Office. An additional fee is charged for this
optional service. All the required forms should be available
through the dissertation office of your university.

Should you choose to copyright your work independently of UMI or without the assistance of your university, you may
register your dissertation by sending the fee (currently $10) and
two copies of the dissertation to the United States Copyright
Office, Library of Congress, Washington, D.C. 20559. Even
though the 1976 Copyright Act states that copyright for your
work is secured automatically when the work is created in fixed
form—that is, being on paper rather than just an idea—infringe-
ment suits cannot ordinarily be filed until a public record of
your copyright is established through formal registration.

Whatever procedure you choose, you are entitled to make
a statement of copyright on a separate page of your dissertation
immediately following the title page.

Once you have successfully completed your dissertation,
thank all those who have helped you. You normally will have
worked most closely with your dissertation director and a few
other readers and advisers whose areas of research or expertise
relate closely to yours. You should give each of these individuals a bound copy of your completed dissertation for their personal libraries. Those who aided you more briefly should be
informed of the completion of your study and offered an abstract of it.

Now, celebrate! Give yourself a party, go on a trip, kiss
your spouse, hug your children, feel proud of your accomplish-
ment. Obtaining a graduate degree may not make you wealthy,
but no one can take away the fact that you have successfully
completed a difficult task and entered the respected community of scholars. Crow a little; you deserve it.

Finally, as you begin your career, don't forget that you
invested a lot of time and effort in completing your thesis or
dissertation. Plan to publish the significant results of your work
within a year of your graduation. Unfortunately, many students
publish nothing after they graduate, and the majority publish an

average of only one article. The world can expect more from you. Don't let it down!

Summary

Your final oral defense is your gateway to the community of scholars. In it, examiners will make a final check on the adequacy of your thesis or dissertation, verify that you personally completed your study, establish that you can synthesize and evaluate data as well as collect it, and demand proof of the thoroughness of your academic preparation and your ability to conduct yourself as a professional.

The examiners in your final oral will usually consist of your dissertation committee plus one or more examiners from outside your department. One of the outsiders will probably be chairperson. You can almost certainly count on your director and probably also on your committee for support, while the outsiders will be more neutral.

Prepare for your oral by learning and following all of your institution's required procedures. You might have friends give you a mock oral, or you might visit the room where the oral will be held and practice giving your summary there. Reading about your topic in recent journals is also a good idea. Enter your examination well rested, well fed, and dressed neatly.

You will probably begin your oral with a fifteen-minute summary of your work. The rest of the time will be devoted to questions and answers. If all goes well, a scholarly discussion of your topic will develop, and you will play a comfortable and professional part in it.

At the end of the oral, you and all visitors will leave the room while the examining committee confers and votes. You will then be called back to hear their decision, which may be pass, fail, or pass with requests for minor or major revisions. If you are passed with a request for major revisions, find out what revisions are required and how you can gain final approval.

After you pass your oral, you may be required to supply an abstract of your dissertation for publication in *Dissertation*

Abstracts International. Your dissertation may also be microfilmed, and you can copyright it if you wish. You should thank all those who helped you in your work and provide the most important of them with copies of your dissertation.

You are sure to feel proud and happy when your months of hard work reach a successful conclusion. Celebrate; then begin looking toward the future. Try to publish the results of your study within a year. Let your completed dissertation become the first step in a long and productive professional career.

 APPENDIX A

A Sample Timeline for Completing a Dissertation

Naturally, all students and all studies are different. Some studies and dissertations can be completed quickly, while others will take much longer. The following timeline, therefore, is intended only as a very approximate guide. Use it as a model to plan your own schedule and to remind yourself of the major steps in the dissertation process. The last step, not shown in the timeline, is publication of your work within one year of completion.

During Coursework

	Semester 1	Semester 2	Semester 3	Semester 4
Become acquainted with library(s) and librarians	⊢—⊣			
Become acquainted with issues and literature in the field	⊢————————————⊣			
Search for dissertation topic		⊢————————⊣		
Search for dissertation director		⊢————⊣		
Choose topic			⊢——⊣	
Choose director			⊢——⊣	
Choose other committee members				⊢—⊣

171

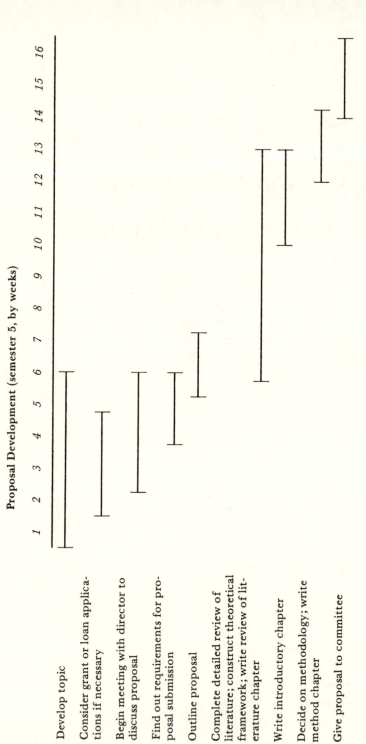

Proposal Development (semester 5, by weeks)

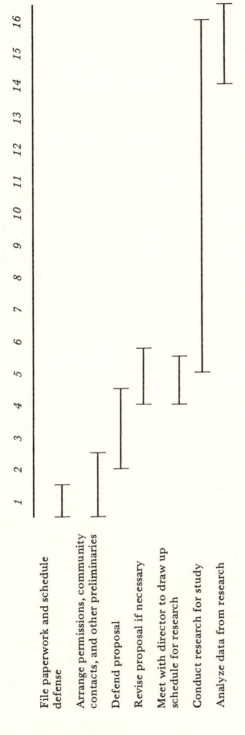

Proposal Defense and Conducting Research (semester 6, by weeks)

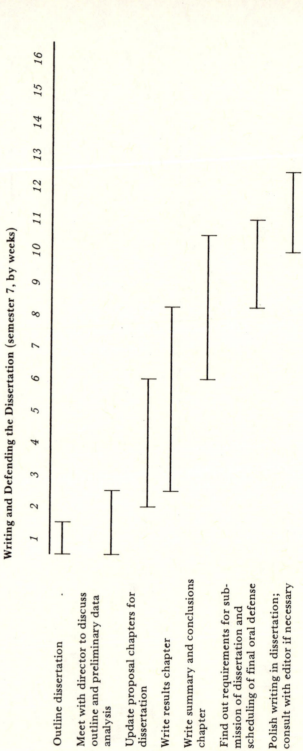

Writing and Defending the Dissertation (semester 7, by weeks)

Submit draft of dissertation to committee

Submit dissertation paperwork and schedule oral defense

Have dissertation professionally typed or printed from word processor

Defend dissertation

Make minor revisions, if necessary

Submit abstract for microfilm and complete other procedures

Graduate

 APPENDIX B

Types of Research

This appendix provides a brief description of six types of research commonly found in dissertations: historical, descriptive, correlational, experimental, causal-comparative, and methodological research. It discusses the format used for each of these research types and offers guidance in conducting studies represented by each type. A more complete description of types of research can be found in most introductory books on research methodology, such as Kerlinger (1973, 1979); Selltiz, Wrightsman, and Cook (1976); and Van Dalen (1979).

Historical Research

Historical research involves the investigation of past events for the purpose of understanding past and present and, to some extent, anticipating the future. This research tests hypotheses about past events by systematically collecting and critically evaluating data concerning them. The steps involved in conducting a historical research study are essentially the same as those for other types of studies, although some special techniques may be used. In general, the historical researcher formulates a problem, collects source materials, criticizes the materials, formulates hypotheses to explain events, and finally interprets and reports his or her findings.

In a historical research study, reviewing the literature and collecting data are part of the same process. Before writing the proposal, some review of the literature is necessary to properly define the problem. Study procedures specified in the proposal would include the further collection, documentation, and analysis of source materials that might be placed in a review of literature in another type of study.

Sources of data in a historical study are classified as primary or secondary sources. Primary sources are accounts of past events by eyewitnesses or actual objects that can be examined directly. Examples of primary sources are original documents, letters, interviews with eyewitnesses, personal records, pictures, and physical remains. Secondary sources consist of information provided by persons who did not directly observe the events. This information may appear in books, periodicals, encyclopedias, or newspapers, or it may come from an interview with someone who has received information about an event from another person. Although a search for evidence may begin by examining secondary sources, the ultimate objective of a historical study is to locate primary sources.

Once sources of historical data are located, they must be carefully scrutinized to determine their authenticity and accuracy. Through the process of *external criticism* the researcher checks the genuineness and integrity of source material by establishing its time, place, and authorship. If the material proves to be authentic, the researcher subjects it to *internal criticism,* which tries to ascertain the meaning and trustworthiness of the data within the material. Some factors that must be considered in internal criticism are the knowledge and competence of the author, time delay between the occurrence and the recording of events, motives of the author, and consistency of the data.

After completing both external and internal criticism of the sources of historical data, the researcher organizes and synthesizes the data in order to explain not only what happened but how and why it happened. Ultimately the researcher forms conclusions about the data and generalizes the findings.

Since the analysis of historical data is primarily logical rather than statistical, historical studies are considered to be qualitative rather than quantitative research. Because of the special nature of historical studies, the format of a historical dissertation may differ substantially from the format presented in this book. In a historical study, the review of literature neces-

sary to define the problem ordinarily is incorporated into the
first chapter of the dissertation instead of being placed in a
separate chapter. Depending on its length, the description of the
methodology could either be a separate chapter or could be a
part of the first chapter. Instead of a single chapter on results,
the historical dissertation ordinarily has from three to five chapters in which the researcher develops the particular themes of
the topic under study. As with other types of dissertations, the
final chapter of a historical dissertation normally has a summary, conclusions, and recommendations for further research;
however, the discussion of the findings would have already been
presented in the previous three to five chapters. For more information on the format of a historical dissertation and for specific
guidance concerning its content, the reader should consult Allen
(1973), Madsen (1983), and Van Dalen (1979).

Examples of historical research are a study of the parallel
development of public and parochial education in Boston from
1900 to 1940, the influence of professional research associations on the shaping of the federal government's policies on
funding behavioral research, and the development of nurses'
unions in the United States and their effect on the professional-
ism of nurses.

Descriptive Research

Descriptive research involves collecting data in order to
answer questions or test hypotheses about the current status of
the situation under study. In the behavioral sciences, most descriptive research can be classified as survey research or observational research.

Survey research typically employs questionnaires or, in
some cases, interviews to determine people's opinions, attitudes,
and perceptions about the situation being studied. Survey research ordinarily uses quantitative methods, but qualitative
methods may be necessary if the data are obtained from interviews. The format of dissertations using survey research would
not differ greatly from that described in this book, and most of

the other guidance presented here is also applicable to survey research studies. Some examples of survey research are an investigation of attitudes of graduate school deans toward having faculty positions that are not on a tenure track, the perceptions of teachers about the effectiveness of open classrooms, and a comparison of criteria used by different accreditation agencies for professional certification.

Observational research determines the current status of a situation by observing it rather than simply asking about it. Observational research can be broadly classified as nonparticipant observation or participant observation. A *case study* is a type of observational research that ordinarily uses nonparticipant observation. In a case study, the researcher performs an in-depth investigation of a situation but usually is not directly involved in the situation and does not control or manipulate it. A case study tries to explain behavior as well as to document it. An example of a case study is the investigation of the socialization of Vietnamese students in a suburban American high school.

Ethnographic research is a type of observational research that usually employs participant observation. Guba and Lincoln (1981) define participant observation as a form of inquiry in which the researcher is both an observer, and as such is responsible to persons outside the situation being studied, and also a genuine participant, and as such has a stake in the situation and its outcomes. Ethnographic research usually occurs in a naturalistic setting; that is, the researcher records and studies behavior as it normally occurs. The ethnographic researcher believes that behavior is significantly influenced by the context or environment in which it occurs and, therefore, that accurate understanding of the behavior requires understanding of that context.

Ethnographic research involves the intensive examination of a situation in which data are collected on many variables over an extended period of time. These data may come from in-depth interviewing, field notes, diaries, thematic musings of the researcher, chronologs (running accounts of behavior, often recorded as episodes occurring at particular times), context maps or diagrams, schedules, taxonomies, sociometrics (relational diagrams showing who interacts with whom), questionnaires, rating scales, checklists, and audio or video recordings. The analysis of these data is largely qualitative. Since the guidance presented in this book deals almost exclusively with quantitative research methods, you should consult other references, such as Bogdan and Biklen (1982), Guba and Lincoln (1981), and Patton (1980), for guidance concerning the analysis and reporting of qualitative data if your dissertation involves ethnographic research.

In addition to being more qualitative than other forms of research, ethnographic research is more inductive. Instead of forming specific hypotheses on the basis of a review of the literature and formally testing these hypotheses with the data using quantitative methods, the ethnographic researcher often forms tentative working hypotheses and strategies that are refined as he or she gains more experience and insight into the situation being studied.

Anthropologists and some sociologists have long used ethnographic research as their primary form of inquiry. The widespread use of this type of research in the other behavioral sciences, especially in educational research, is more recent. Today most graduate programs have courses in qualitative methods or devote a substantial portion of the traditional research methods course to these methods. As its popularity has grown, ethnographic research is being used more often by researchers with training in traditional quantitative methods. The result has been the emergence of a modified ethnographic approach (Gay, 1981) that is more structured than the traditional method. For example, the traditional approach of going into the field and allowing the issues to emerge has given way to the specification of hypotheses that are tested by data obtained by the researcher while observing specific activities.

Examples of ethnographic research are an examination of the culture of an eleventh-grade social studies class in a midwestern suburban high school where the researcher participates as a member of the class on a daily basis, and a study of the pressures involved in critical care nursing where the researcher is a nurse assigned to an intensive care unit in a hospital.

Correlational Research

Correlational research involves collecting data to determine the existence of a relationship between two or more variables and to estimate the relationship's magnitude. The relationship is usually described by a statistic called the Pearson Product-Moment Correlation Coefficient or, simply Pearson's r or the correlation coefficient. This number, which is between -1.00 and 1.00, describes the extent of a linear relationship between two variables—that is, how closely the points represented by ordered pairs of individuals' scores on each variable approximate a straight line when graphed in a coordinate system. Values of -1.00 and 1.00 indicate a perfect linear relationship (inverse and direct, respectively), while a value of .00 indicates no linear relationship. Generally the strength of the linear relationship is measured by squaring the correlation coefficient. Most introductory statistics textbooks, such as Glass and Hopkins (1984), Hays (1981), and Shavelson (1981), describe the properties of the correlation coefficient as well as provide a description of other indexes of relationship.

Correlational research studies are usually classified as relationship studies or prediction studies. *Relationship studies* examine the association between measures of different variables obtained at approximately the same time. In addition to investigating relationships between variables of interest, these studies often try to obtain a better understanding of factors that make up a complex construct such as intelligence, self-concept, or school ability. Relationship studies also are often done as a preliminary to causal-comparative and experimental studies (discussed later in this appendix) in order to identify important variables that the researcher may want to include in the design of the later studies.

Prediction studies involve the establishment of an equation that is used to predict future performance on some variable, called the dependent variable or the criterion, from information obtained from other variables, called the independent variables or the predictors. In addition to predicting performance on the criterion, researchers often seek to identify which predictors are most important in explaining changes in the criterion. Prediction studies are used to aid in the selection or placement of individuals, to identify individuals to perform certain tasks or to receive special services, to determine the criterion-related or predictive validity of measuring instruments, and to test hypotheses concerning variables believed to be predictors of a given criterion.

Correlational research studies normally employ quantitative methods, so a dissertation involving correlational research would use the format described in this book. In fact, the guidance provided in this book applies particularly well to correlational research.

Examples of correlational research studies include predicting achievement from measures of self-concept and locus of control (prediction study), a factor analysis of the Rome Patient Sensitivity Scale (relationship study), changes in social perspective-taking ability of children as a function of age (relationship study), and the relative importance of home variables, school variables, and personal variables in predicting success in school (prediction study).

Experimental Research

Experimental research involves examination of the effects of at least one independent variable on one or more dependent variables while other relevant variables are controlled. Direct manipulation of at least one independent variable is the main characteristic that differentiates experimental research from other methods. When well conducted, experimental studies provide the strongest evidence for cause-and-effect relationships. Kerlinger (1979) states that experimental research fulfills the ideal of science by addressing research questions less ambiguously than other methods of research.

Control of extraneous variables is essential in experimental research studies. The researcher tries to remove the influence of any variable, other than the independent variables of interest, that might affect the dependent variable. Variables that typically need to be controlled are those involving individual differences among subjects, such as ability or interest or readiness, and environmental variables, such as teachers or instructional programs or home experiences. Such variables may produce unwanted differences between experimental groups. Uncontrolled extraneous variables that affect performance on the dependent variables increase the chances of experimental error and jeopardize the experiment's validity.

A good research design maximizes both the internal validity and the external validity of an experiment. *Internal validity* is the extent to which changes in the dependent variable can be attributed to changes in an independent variable. *External validity* refers to the generalizability or representativeness of the findings. Campbell and Stanley (1966) provide an extensive treatment of threats to internal and external validity of experiments and suggest designs that control for these threats. Their monograph should be required reading for you if you are planning to conduct an experimental study.

One way to control for extraneous variables is through randomization. Randomization primarily refers to the random assignment of individuals to experimental conditions. Ideally, random assignment should follow random selection of the sample from the population. Random assignment is the primary way of reducing initial differences between groups. Experimental designs in which random assignment to groups is not possible are called quasi-experimental. An excellent discussion of quasi-experimental designs and other issues involved with research in field settings is provided by Cook and Campbell (1979).

A second way to control for extraneous variables is to hold them constant. Including only male subjects removes the effect of sex from the dependent variable, for example. Ensuring that all experimental conditions, such as time of day, physical appearance of the room, and directions to the subjects, are identical removes them as potential sources of variation.

Extraneous variables can also be controlled for by introducing them directly into the design and including them as sources of variation in the statistical model used to analyze the data. For example, the use of blocking variables in the analysis of variance, covariates in the analysis of covariance, and predictors entered prior to other independent variables in regression analysis provides statistical control for the variables involved.

Experimental research studies are normally considered to be quantitative because of the frequent use of descriptive and inferential statistics in the analysis of data from such studies. The format of the dissertation and the specific guidance concerning each section as presented in this book are particularly applicable to experimental studies.

Some examples of experimental research are a study of the instructional effectiveness of different discovery methods in which the discovery conditions are operationally defined and manipulated by the researcher and subjects are randomly assigned to each experimental condition; the influence of the perceived warmth of counselors on the counselors' perceived effectiveness; and the relative effectiveness of three types of therapy on overcoming fears and phobias.

Causal-Comparative Research

Often a researcher seeks to provide evidence for cause-and-effect relationships by examining the effect of one or more variables on another variable, without being able to manipulate any of the variables. This type of research is called causal-comparative. Causal-comparative research occurs frequently in the behavioral sciences because the manipulation of many variables, such as personality traits, race, handicaps, ability, smoking, diseases, and home experiences, is impossible, impractical, or unethical. Causal-comparative research appears similar to experimental research because of the cause-and-effect questions raised, but it is actually a form of descriptive research and is classified as such by several authors (Van Dalen, 1979; Best, 1981).

Causal-comparative research is also referred to as *ex post facto* research, since both the effect and the alleged cause have already occurred and are studied by the researcher "after the fact." Typically a researcher observes groups that differ in some variable (the alleged effect) and attempts to identify factors that have led to this difference. Unlike the experimental researcher, the causal-comparative researcher does not manipulate any variables and is not able to randomly assign subjects to groups formed by combinations of these variables. Because of the researcher's inability to do these things, causal-comparative research designs are also referred to as nonexperimental designs (Pedhazur, 1982).

The following example is typical of causal-comparative research. In attempting to explain differences in the reading performance of first graders, a researcher might hypothesize that parents reading to the child at home for thirty minutes or more each day is the major contributing factor. To test this hypothesis, the researcher could select a group of first graders whose parents read to them every day for thirty minutes or more and a group whose parents don't do this. If the group whose parents do read to them every day for at least thirty minutes has higher reading performance, then the researcher's hypothesis apparently would be supported. Alternatively, the researcher could select a group of better readers and a group of poorer readers and determine the number of children in each group whose parents read to them at least thirty minutes each day. If this number is higher in the better readers' group, then once again the researcher's hypothesis apparently would be supported.

However, researchers need to recognize two important limitations of causal-comparative research that may make the interpretation of such studies very difficult. First, since the independent variables cannot be manipulated, the researcher must be content with analyzing the association between the presumed cause and the alleged effect. An association between variables is not sufficient evidence of causality. In the preceding example, since both differences in reading performance and in parent practices about reading to their children occurred prior to the study, the resulting association provides necessary but not sufficient evidence of causation. Both factors might stem from a higher parental education level or a genetic intelligence factor, for example. Furthermore, a researcher cannot determine simply by examining the association between these two variables whether different parent practices produce or are the result of differences in reading performance.

Second, since subjects cannot be randomly assigned to groups, control over other relevant variables is seriously restricted. Groups that have already been established may differ on other important variables that contribute to differences on the variables of interest. The issue here basically is proper model specification. In our example, only differences in parent practices were considered as contributing to differences in reading achievement. Other variables not considered by the researcher, such as preschool experiences or the verbal aptitude of individual students, may have contributed as much or more. Causes are often multiple, and omitting important variables from the model used to represent the research situation may produce a spurious relationship between the variables considered and lead to misinterpretation of a study's findings.

Ordinarily the methods used to analyze data from a causal-comparative study are the same as those used to analyze data from an experimental research study. Thus the dissertation format and special guidance presented in this book are applicable to causal-comparative dissertations as well as to experimental ones.

Some additional examples of causal-comparative studies are an investigation of whether smoking is a factor in the development of lung cancer, an examination of factors contributing to different dropout rates among black and white urban secondary school students, and a comparison of the language development of hearing-impaired students with hearing parents to the language development of hearing-impaired students with hearing-impaired parents.

Methodological Research

Methodological research involves investigation of the theoretical and applied aspects of statistics, measurement, evaluation, and ways of obtaining and analyzing data (Kerlinger, 1979). Often this type of research uses the methodology of experimental research; however, in some cases, this research involves theoretical investigations that do not easily fit into any of the research categories previously discussed. The format of dissertations for studies in this latter group may differ somewhat from the format given in this book. Such dissertations ordinarily need additional chapters to develop the theoretical models being examined or to discuss different implications of these models. Examples of methodological research are a comparison of the relative effectiveness of three evaluation models for detecting effective and ineffective nursing homes, a comparison of different methods for estimating the reliability of criterion-referenced tests, and an examination of the robustness of the analysis of covariance when critical assumptions are violated.

 APPENDIX C

Additional Resources for Dissertation and Thesis Writers

Directories of Funding Sources

Foundation Grants to Individuals. New York: The Foundation Center, 1982.

Grants Magazine: The Journal of Sponsored Research and Other Programs. New York: Plenum, 1978–. (quarterly)

Lowman, R. P., Holt, V. E., and O'Bryant, C. (eds.). *American Psychological Association's Guide to Research Support.* Washington, D.C.: American Psychological Association, 1981.

Searles, A., and Scott, A. *Guide to Financial Aids for Students in Arts and Sciences for Graduate and Professional Study.* (Rev. ed.) New York: ARCO Publishing, 1974.

UNESCO. *Study Abroad: International Scholarships, International Courses.* Paris: UNESCO. (biennial)

Wilson, W. K. (ed.). *Directory of Research Grants 1985.* Phoenix, Ariz.: The Oryx Press, 1985.

On-line Data Bases of Funding Sources

Foundation Directory. New York: Foundation Center. (Available through **DIALOG**)

Foundation Grants Index. New York: Foundation Center. (Available through **DIALOG**)

Grant Information System. Phoenix, Ariz.: Oryx Press. (Available through ORBIT)

Form and Style Manuals

Flesch, R., and Lass, A. *A New Guide to Better Writing.* New York: Popular Library, 1977.

Follett, W. *Modern American Usage: A Guide.* New York: Hill and Wang, 1979.

Goeller, C. *Writing to Communicate.* New York: New American Library, 1975.

Guthrie, L. O. *Factual Communication.* New York: Macmillan, 1953.

Murdock, M. *Writing Clearly and Effectively.* Washington, D.C.: Transemantics, Inc., 1981.

Swartz, R. J. *Starting Point: A Guide to Basic Writing Skills.* Englewood Cliffs, N.J.: Prentice-Hall, 1980.

Underwood, V., and Kett, M. *College Writing Skills.* (2nd ed.) Columbus, Ohio: Merrill, 1981.

A Selected Bibliography of Statistical Procedures

Interpreting Statistics

Huck, S. W., Cormier, W. H., and Bounds, W. G. *Reading Statistics and Research.* New York: Harper & Row, 1974.

Elementary Statistics

Glass, G. V., and Hopkins, K. D. *Statistical Methods in Education and Psychology.* (2nd ed.) Englewood Cliffs, N.J.: Prentice-Hall, 1984.

Glass, G. V., and Stanley, J. C. *Statistical Methods in Education and Psychology.* Englewood Cliffs, N.J.: Prentice-Hall, 1970.

Hays, W. L. *Statistics.* (3rd ed.) New York: Holt, Rinehart & Winston, 1981.

Shavelson, R. J. *Statistical Reasoning for the Behavioral Sciences.* Newton, Mass.: Allyn & Bacon, 1981.

Design and Analysis of Variance

Kirk, R. E. *Experimental Design: Procedures for the Behavioral Sciences.* (2nd ed.) Monterey, Calif.: Brooks/Cole, 1982.
Winer, B. J. *Statistical Principles in Experimental Design.* (2nd ed.) New York: McGraw-Hill, 1971.

Regression Analysis

Cohen, J., and Cohen, P. *Applied Multiple Regression/Correlation for the Behavioral Sciences.* Hillsdale, N.J.: Erlbaum, 1975.
Pedhazur, E. J. *Multiple Regression in Behavioral Research: Explanation and Prediction.* (2nd ed.) New York: Holt, Rinehart & Winston, 1982.

Nonparametric Statistics

Siegel, S. *Nonparametric Statistics for the Behavioral Sciences.* New York: McGraw-Hill, 1956.

Multivariate Statistics

Lorr, M. *Cluster Analysis for Social Scientists: Techniques for Analyzing and Simplifying Complex Blocks of Data.* San Francisco: Jossey-Bass, 1983.
Marascuilo, L. A., and Levin, J. R. *Multivariate Statistics in the Social Sciences: A Researcher's Guide.* Monterey, Calif.: Brooks/Cole, 1983.
Rummel, R. J. *Applied Factor Analysis.* Evanston, Ill.: Northwestern University Press, 1970.
Thorndike, R. M. *Correlational Procedures for Research.* New York: Gardner Press, 1978.
Timm, N. H. *Multivariate Analysis with Applications in Education and Psychology.* Monterey, Calif.: Brooks/Cole, 1975.

Structural Equations/Causal Models

Bentler, P. M. "Multivariate Analysis with Latent Variables: Causal Modeling." In M. R. Rosenzweig and L. W. Porter (eds.), *Annual Review of Psychology*. Vol. 31. Palo Alto, Calif.: Annual Reviews, 1980.
Kenny, D. A. *Correlation and Causality*. New York: Wiley, 1979.

Time-Series Analysis

Gottman, J. M. *Time-Series Analysis: A Comprehensive Introduction for Social Scientists*. New York: Cambridge University Press, 1981.

Simultaneous Inference Procedures

Miller, R. G. *Simultaneous Inference Procedures*. (2nd ed.) New York: McGraw-Hill, 1981.

Contingency Table Analysis/Log-Linear Models

Bishop, Y. M. M., Feinberg, S. E., and Holland, P. W. *Discrete Multivariate Analysis: Theory and Practice*. Cambridge, Mass.: MIT Press, 1975.
Feinberg, S. E. *The Analysis of Cross-Classified Categorical Data*. Cambridge, Mass.: MIT Press, 1977.
Kennedy, J. J. *Analyzing Qualitative Data: Introductory Log-Linear Analysis for Behavioral Research*. New York: Praeger, 1983.

References

Abstracts for Social Workers. Washington, D.C.: National Association of Social Workers, 1965-1977.

Abstracts in Anthropology. Westport, Conn.: Greenwood Press, 1970-.

Abstracts of Instructional and Research Materials in Vocational and Technical Education. Columbus, Ohio: Center for Vocational and Technical Education, 1967-.

Acronyms, Initialisms, and Abbreviations Dictionary. (8th ed.) Detroit: Gale Research Co., 1983-1984.

Allen, G. R. *The Graduate Students' Guide to Theses and Dissertations: A Practical Manual for Writing and Research.* San Francisco: Jossey-Bass, 1973.

American Psychological Association. *Principles for the Care and Use of Animals.* Washington, D.C.: American Psychological Association, 1971.

American Psychological Association. *Ethical Principles in the Conduct of Research with Human Participants.* Washington, D.C.: American Psychological Association, 1982.

American Psychological Association. *Publication Manual.* (3rd ed.) Washington, D.C.: American Psychological Association, 1983.

American Statistics Index: A Comprehensive Guide and Index to the Statistical Publications of the U.S. Government. Washington, D.C.: Congressional Information Service, 1973-.

Annual Register of Grant Support. Chicago: Marquis Who's Who, 1969-.

Annual Review of Anthropology. Palo Alto, Calif.: Annual Reviews, 1972-.

Annual Review of Psychology. Palo Alto, Calif.: Annual Reviews, 1950-.

Annual Review of Sociology. Palo Alto, Calif.: Annual Reviews, 1975-.

Arieti, S. (ed.) *American Handbook of Psychiatry.* (3 vols.) (2nd ed.) New York: Wiley, 1974.

Ash, L. (Comp.) *Subject Collections: A Guide to Special Book Collections and Subject Emphases as Reported by University, College, Public, and Special Libraries, and Museums in the United States and Canada.* (6th ed.) New York: Bowker, 1985.

Ausubel, D. P. "The Use of Advance Organizers in the Learning and Retention of Meaningful Verbal Material." *Journal of Educational Psychology,* 1960, *51,* 267-272.

Basic Facts and Figures: International Statistics Relating to Education, Culture, and Mass Communication. Paris: UNESCO, 1952-1961.

Bauer, D. G. *The "How To" Grants Manual: Successful Grant-seeking Techniques for Obtaining Public and Private Grants.* New York: American Council on Education and Macmillan, 1984.

Beere, C. A. *Women and Women's Issues: A Handbook of Tests and Measures.* San Francisco: Jossey-Bass, 1979.

Berk, R. A. (ed.) *Criterion-Referenced Measurement: The State of the Art.* Baltimore, Md.: Johns Hopkins University Press, 1980.

Best, J. W. *Research in Education.* (4th ed.) Englewood Cliffs, N.J.: Prentice-Hall, 1981.

Bibliographic Index: A Cumulative Bibliography of Bibliographies. New York: H. W. Wilson, 1938-.

Bogdan, R. C., and Biklen, S. K. *Qualitative Research for Education: An Introduction to Theory and Methods.* Newton, Mass.: Allyn & Bacon, 1982.

Books in Print. New York: Bowker, 1948-.

Borgatta, E. F., and Lambert, W. W. (eds.) *Handbook of Personality Theory and Research.* Chicago: Rand McNally, 1968.

Boyer, E. G. (ed.) *Measures of Maturation: An Anthology of Early Childhood Observation Instruments.* (3 vols.) Philadelphia: Research for Better Schools, 1973.

Brennan, R. L. *Elements of Generalizability Theory.* Iowa City, Iowa: American College Testing Program, 1983.

Buros, O. K. *Mental Measurements Yearbook of the School of Education; Rutgers University.* New Brunswick, N.J.: Rutgers University Press, 1938.

Buros, O. K. *Mental Measurements Yearbook.* Highland Park, N.J.: Mental Measurements Yearbook, 1940.

Buros, O. K. *Mental Measurements Yearbook.* Highland Park, N.J.: Rutgers University Press, 1949.

Buros, O. K. *Mental Measurements Yearbook.* Highland Park, N.J.: Gryphon Press, 1953.

Buros, O. K. *Mental Measurements Yearbook.* Highland Park, N.J.: Gryphon Press, 1959.

Buros, O. K. *Mental Measurements Yearbook.* Highland Park, N.J.: Gryphon Press, 1965.

Buros, O. K. *Mental Measurements Yearbook.* Highland Park, N.J.: Gryphon Press, 1972.

Buros, O. K. *Mental Measurements Yearbook.* Highland Park, N.J.: Gryphon Press, 1978.

Campbell, D. T., and Fiske, D. W. "Convergent and Discriminant Validation by the Multitrait-Multimethod Matrix." *Psychological Bulletin,* 1959, *56,* 81–105.

Campbell, D. T., and Stanley, J. C. *Experimental and Quasi-Experimental Designs for Research.* Chicago: Rand McNally, 1966.

Campbell, W. G., Ballou, S. V., and Slade, C. *Form and Style: Theses, Reports, Term Papers.* Boston: Houghton Mifflin, 1982.

Chicago, University of. *A Manual of Style.* (13th ed.) Chicago: University of Chicago Press, 1982.

Child Development Abstracts and Bibliography. Washington, D.C.: National Research Council, Committee on Child Development, 1927–.

Chun, K., Cobb, S., and French, J. R. *Measures for Psychological Assessment: A Guide to 3,000 Original Sources and Their Applications.* Ann Arbor, Mich.: Survey Research Center, Institute for Social Research, 1975.

Cochran, W. G. *Sampling Techniques.* (3rd ed.) New York: Wiley, 1977.

Cohen, J. *Statistical Power Analysis for the Behavioral Sciences.* New York: Academic Press, 1969.

The College Blue Book: Scholarships, Fellowships, Grants and Loans. (19th ed.) New York: Macmillan Information, 1983.

Comprehensive Dissertation Index, 1861-1972. Ann Arbor, Mich.: Xerox University Microfilms, 1973 and Supplements.

Compton, C. *A Guide to 65 Diagnostic Tests for Special Education.* Belmont, Calif.: Fearon-Pitman, 1979.

Cook, T. D., and Campbell, D. T. *Quasi-Experimentation: Design and Analysis Issues for Field Settings.* Chicago: Rand McNally, 1979.

Cronbach, L. J. "Test Validation." In R. L. Thorndike (ed.), *Educational Measurement.* (2nd ed.) Washington, D.C.: American Council on Education, 1971.

Cronbach, L. J., and others. *The Dependability of Behavioral Measurements: Theory of Generalizability for Scores and Profiles.* New York: Wiley, 1972.

Cumulative Book Index. New York: Bowker, 1933-.

Current Index to Journals in Education. New York: Macmillan; Phoenix, Ariz.: Oryx Press, 1969-.

Dissertation Abstracts International. Ann Arbor, Mich.: Xerox University Microfilms, 1952-.

Dixon, W. J., and Brown, M. B. (eds.) *BMDP Statistical Software.* Berkeley: University of California Press, 1983.

Education Index. New York: H. W. Wilson, 1932-.

Educational Administration Abstracts. Columbus, Ohio: University Council for Educational Administration, 1966-.

Educational Testing Service. *Tests in Microfiche.* Princeton, N.J.: Educational Testing Service, 1975-.

Encyclopedia of Associations. (3 vols.) (17th ed.) Detroit: Gale Research, Co., 1982.

Encyclopedia of Education. (10 vols.) New York: Macmillan, 1971.

Encyclopedia of Educational Research. (4 vols.) (5th ed.) Riverside, N.J.: Macmillan Professional and Library Services for the American Educational Research Association, 1982.

Encyclopedia of Social Work. (17th ed.) Washington, D.C.: National Association of Social Workers, 1977.

Exceptional Child Education Resources. Reston, Va.: Council for Exceptional Children, 1969-.

Eysenck, H. J. (Ed.) *Handbook of Abnormal Psychology.* (2nd ed.) San Diego, Calif.: R. R. Knapp, 1973.

Eysenck, H. J., and Arnold, W. *Encyclopedia of Psychology.* (3 vols.) New York: Herder and Herder, 1972.

Family Educational Rights and Privacy Act. 20 *U.S. Code,* sec. 12, 32G (1976).

Forthcoming Books: A Forecast of Books to Come. New York: Bowker, 1966-.

The Foundation Directory. (8th ed.) New York: Foundation Center, 1981.

Fowler, H. W. *Dictionary of Modern English Usage.* (2nd ed.) Edited by E. Gowers. New York: Oxford University Press, 1965.

Frick, T., and Semmel, M. I. "Observer Agreement and Reliabilities of Classroom Observational Measures." *Review of Educational Research,* 1979, *48,* 157-184.

Friedman, M., and Ulmer, D. *Treating Type A Behavior—and Your Heart.* New York: Knopf, 1984.

Fryer, D. H., and Henry, E. R. (Eds.) (2 vols.) *Handbook of Applied Psychology.* New York: Holt, Rinehart and Winston, 1950.

Gagne, R. M. *The Conditions of Learning.* (3rd ed.) New York: Holt, Rinehart and Winston, 1977.

Garfield, S. L., and Bergin, A. E. (eds.) *Handbook of Psychotherapy and Behavior Change: An Empirical Analysis.* (2nd ed.) New York: Wiley, 1978.

Gay, L. R. *Educational Research: Competencies for Analysis and Application.* (2nd ed.) Columbus, Ohio: Merrill, 1981.

Glass, G. V., and Hopkins, K. D. *Statistical Methods in Education and Psychology.* (2nd ed.) Englewood Cliffs, N.J.: Prentice-Hall, 1984.

Glass, G. V., and Stanley, J. C. *Statistical Methods in Educa-*

tion and Psychology. Englewood Cliffs, N.J.: Prentice-Hall, 1970.

Good, C. V. *Dictionary of Education.* (3rd ed.) New York: McGraw-Hill, 1973.

Gould, J., and Kolb, W. L. (eds.) *A Dictionary of the Social Sciences.* New York: Free Press of Glencoe, 1964.

Grants Register, 1985–1987. (9th ed.) New York: St. Martin's Press, 1984.

Gronlund, N. E. *Constructing Achievement Tests.* (3rd ed.) Englewood Cliffs, N.J.: Prentice-Hall, 1982.

Guba, E. G., and Lincoln, Y. S. *Effective Evaluation: Improving the Usefulness of Evaluation Results Through Responsive and Naturalistic Approaches.* San Francisco: Jossey-Bass, 1981.

Guertin, W. H., and Bailey, J. P. *Introduction to Modern Factor Analysis.* Ann Arbor, Mich.: Edwards, 1970.

Guilford, J. P. *Psychometric Methods.* (2nd ed.) New York: McGraw-Hill, 1954.

Hare, A. P. *Handbook of Small Group Research.* (2nd ed.) New York: Free Press, 1976.

Hays, W. L. *Statistics.* (3rd ed.) New York: Holt, Rinehart & Winston, 1981.

Helwig, J. T., and Council, K. A. (eds.) *SAS User's Guide.* Raleigh, N.C.: SAS Institute, 1979.

International Encyclopedia of Higher Education. (10 vols.) San Francisco: Jossey-Bass, 1977.

The International Encyclopedia of Psychiatry, Psychology, Psychoanalysis, and Neurology. New York: Van Nostrand Reinhold, 1977.

International Encyclopedia of the Social Sciences. (17 vols.) New York: Macmillan, 1968.

Johnson, O. G. *Tests and Measurements in Child Development: A Handbook.* San Francisco: Jossey-Bass, 1971.

Johnson, O. G. *Tests and Measurements in Child Development: Handbook II.* (2 vols.) San Francisco: Jossey-Bass, 1976.

Journal of Counseling Psychology. Washington, D.C.: American Psychological Association, 1954–.

Journal of Educational Measurement. East Lansing, Mich.: National Council on Measurement in Education, 1964–.

Kerlinger, F. N. *Foundations of Behavioral Research.* (2nd ed.) New York: Holt, Rinehart & Winston, 1973.

Kerlinger, F. N. *Behavioral Research: A Conceptual Approach.* New York: Holt, Rinehart & Winston, 1979.

Kirk, R. E. *Experimental Design: Procedures for the Behavioral Sciences.* (2nd ed.) Monterey, Calif.: Brooks/Cole, 1982.

Koelle, W. H. "The Effects of Locus of Control and Self-Concept on Academic Achievement in Deaf Adolescents Using Instrumentation Modified for Deaf Subjects." Unpublished doctoral dissertation, School of Education, The Catholic University of America, 1981.

Lake, D. G., Miles, M. B., and Earle, R. B. *Measuring Human Behavior: Tools for the Assessment of Social Functioning.* New York: Teachers College Press, 1973.

Language and Language Behavior Abstracts. Ann Arbor: Center for Research on Language and Language Behavior, University of Michigan, 1967-.

Lindzey, G., and Aronson, E. (eds.) *The Handbook of Social Psychology.* (5 vols.) (2nd ed.) Reading, Mass.: Addison-Wesley, 1968-1970.

McLaughlin, B. "An Experimental Comparison of Discovery and Didactic Computerized Instructional Strategies in the Learning of Computer Programming." Unpublished doctoral dissertation, School of Education, The Catholic University of America, 1981.

Madsen, D. *Successful Dissertations and Theses: A Guide to Graduate Student Research from Proposal to Completion.* San Francisco: Jossey-Bass, 1983.

Marascuilo, L. A. *Statistical Methods for Behavioral Science Research.* New York: McGraw-Hill, 1971.

Mauser, A. J. *Assessing the Learning Disabled: Selected Instruments.* San Rafael, Calif.: Academic Therapy Publications, 1977.

Miller, R. G. *Simultaneous Inference Procedures.* (2nd ed.) New York: Springer-Verlag, 1981.

Mussen, P. H. (Ed.) *Carmichael's Manual of Child Psychology.* (2 vols.) (3rd ed.) New York: Wiley, 1970.

National Society for Medical Research. "Principles of Laboratory Animal Care." Washington, D.C.: National Society for Medical Research, n.d.

New Research Centers. (3 issues per year.) Detroit: Gale Research Co.

News on Tests. Princeton, N.J.: Educational Testing Service, 1982-.

Nunnally, J. C. *Psychometric Theory.* (2nd ed.) New York: McGraw-Hill, 1978.

Partridge, E. *Concise Usage and Abusage: A Modern Guide to Good English.* New York: Philosophical Library, 1954.

Patton, M. Q. *Qualitative Evaluation Methods.* Beverly Hills, Calif.: Sage, 1980.

Pedhazur, E. J. *Multiple Regression in Behavioral Research: Explanation and Prediction.* New York: Holt, Rinehart & Winston, 1982.

Perrin, P. G. *Writer's Guide and Index to English.* (6th ed.) Edited by W. R. Ebbitt and D. R. Ebbit. Glenview, Ill.: Scott, Foresman, 1978.

Popham, W. J. *Criterion-Referenced Measurement.* Englewood Cliffs, N.J.: Prentice-Hall, 1978.

The Psychoanalytic Study of the Child. New York: International Press, 1945-.

Psychological Abstracts. Washington, D.C.: American Psychological Association, 1927-.

Public Affairs Information Service Bulletin. New York: Public Affairs Information Service, 1915-.

Raj, D. *The Design of Sample Surveys.* New York: McGraw-Hill, 1972.

Research Centers Directory. (7th ed.) Detroit: Gale Research Co., 1982.

Resources in Education. Washington, D.C.: U.S. Government Printing Office, 1966-.

Review of Child Development Research. (5 vols.) Chicago: University of Chicago Press, 1970-1975.

Review of Educational Research. Washington, D.C.: American Educational Research Association, 1931-.

Review of Research in Education. Edited by F. N. Kerlinger. Itasca, Ill.: F. E. Peacock, for the American Educational Research Association, 1973-.

Roget, P. M. *Roget's International Thesaurus.* (4th ed.) New York: Crowell, 1977.

Schatzman, L., and Strauss, A. *Field Research: Strategies for a National Sociology.* Englewood Cliffs, N.J.: Prentice-Hall, 1973.

Scholars' Guide to Washington, D.C. for African Studies. Edited by P. M. Bhatt. Washington, D.C.: Smithsonian Institution Press, 1980.

Scholars' Guide to Washington, D.C. for Central and East European Studies. Edited by K. J. Dillon. Washington, D.C.: Smithsonian Institution Press, 1980.

Scholars' Guide to Washington, D.C. for East Asian Studies. Edited by H. N. Kim. Washington, D.C.: Smithsonian Institution Press, 1979.

Scholars' Guide to Washington, D.C. for Latin American and Caribbean Studies. Edited by M. Grow. Washington, D.C.: Smithsonian Institution Press, 1979.

Scholars' Guide to Washington, D.C. for Middle Eastern Studies. Edited by S. R. Dorr. Washington, D.C.: Smithsonian Institution Press, 1981.

Scholars' Guide to Washington, D.C. for Northwest European Studies. Edited by L. A. Pitschman. Washington, D.C.: Smithsonian Institution Press, 1984.

Scholars' Guide to Washington, D.C. for Russian/Soviet Studies. Edited by S. A. Grant. Washington, D.C.: Smithsonian Institution Press, 1977.

Scholars' Guide to Washington, D.C. for South Asian Studies. Edited by E. Rahim. Washington, D.C.: Smithsonian Institution Press, 1981.

Scholars' Guide to Washington, D.C. for Southeast Asian Studies. Edited by P. M. Mayerchak. Washington, D.C.: Smithsonian Institution Press, 1983.

Selltiz, C., Wrightsman, L. S., and Cook, S. W. *Research Methods in Social Relations.* (3rd ed.) New York: Holt, Rinehart & Winston, 1976.

Shavelson, R. J. *Statistical Reasoning for the Behavioral Sciences.* Newton, Mass.: Allyn & Bacon, 1981.

Shaw, M. E., and Wright, J. W. *Scales for the Measurement of Attitudes.* New York: McGraw-Hill, 1967.

Sheehy, E. P. (Comp.) *Guide to Reference Books*. (9th ed.) Chicago: American Library Association, 1976.

Sheehy, E. P. (comp.) *Guide to Reference Books: Supplements*. (9th ed.) Chicago: American Library Association, 1980, 1982.

Social Sciences and Humanities Index. New York: H. W. Wilson, 1965–1974.

Social Sciences Citation Index: An International Multidisciplinary Index to the Literature of the Social, Behavioral, and Related Sciences. Philadelphia: Institute for Scientific Information, 1967–.

Social Sciences Index. New York: H. W. Wilson, 1974–.

Social Work Research and Abstracts. Washington, D.C.: National Association of Social Workers, 1977–.

Sociological Abstracts. New York: Sociological Abstracts, 1953–.

Sociological Review. Staffordshire: University of Keele, 1953–.

Spradley, J. P. *The Ethnographic Interview*. New York: Holt, Rinehart & Winston, 1979.

Spradley, J. P. *Participant Observation*. New York: Holt, Rinehart & Winston, 1980.

SPSS, Inc. *SPSS X: A Complete Guide to SPSS Language and Operations*. New York: McGraw-Hill, 1983.

Statistical Yearbook. Paris: UNESCO, 1964–.

Strunk, W., and White, E. B. *Elements of Style* (3rd ed.) New York: Macmillan, 1979.

Subject Guide to Books in Print. (2 vols.) New York: Bowker.

Sweetland, R. C. *Tests: A Comprehensive Reference for Assessments in Psychology, Education, and Business*. Kansas City, Mo.: Test Corporation of America, 1984.

Tuckman, B. W. *Conducting Educational Research*. New York: Harcourt Brace Jovanovich, 1972.

Tukey, J. W. *Exploratory Data Analysis*. Reading, Mass.: Addison-Wesley, 1977.

Turabian, K. L. *A Manual for Writers of Term Papers, Theses, and Dissertations*. (4th ed.) Chicago: University of Chicago Press, 1973.

U.S. Bureau of the Census. *Statistical Abstract of the United States*. Washington, D.C.: U.S. Government Printing Office, 1878–.

U.S. Library of Congress, Subject Cataloging Division. *Library of Congress Subject Headings.* (2 vols.) (9th ed.) Washington, D.C.: Library of Congress, 1980.

U.S. National Center for Education Statistics. *Projections of Educational Statistics.* Washington, D.C.: U.S. Government Printing Office, 1964–.

U.S. National Center for Education Statistics. *The Condition of Education.* Washington, D.C.: U.S. Government Printing Office, 1975–.

U.S. National Center for Education Statistics. *Digest of Educational Statistics.* Washington, D.C.: U.S. Government Printing Office, 1982.

Van Dalen, D. B. *Understanding Educational Research.* (4th ed.) New York: McGraw-Hill, 1979.

Wainer, H., and Thissen, D. "Graphical Data Analysis." *Annual Review of Psychology,* 1981, *32,* 191–241.

Wilkening, H. E. *The Psychology Almanac: A Handbook for Students.* Monterey, Calif.: Brooks/Cole, 1973.

Williams, B. *A Sampler on Sampling.* New York: Wiley, 1978.

Winer, B. J. *Statistical Principles in Experimental Design.* (2nd ed.) New York: McGraw-Hill, 1971.

Wittrock, M. (ed.) *Third Handbook of Research on Teaching.* Riverside, N.J.: Macmillan Professional and Library Services for the American Educational Research Association, in press.

Wolman, B. B. (ed.) *Handbook of Clinical Psychology.* New York: McGraw-Hill, 1965.

Wolman, B. B. (ed.) *Dictionary of Behavioral Science.* New York: Van Nostrand Reinhold, 1973.

World Survey of Education. (5 vols.) Paris: UNESCO, 1955–1972.

The Yearbook of Psychiatry and Applied Mental Health. Chicago: Year Book Medical Publishers, 1970–.

Index